EVERYONE'S A TEACHER

A universal methodology for transferring knowledge with extraordinary outcomes

MARIA DOYLE

First published in 2025 by Maria Doyle

© Maria Doyle
The moral rights of the author have been asserted.

All rights reserved. Except as permitted under the Australian Copyright Act 1968 (for example, a fair dealing for the purposes of study, research, criticism or review), no part of this book may be reproduced, stored in a retrieval system, communicated or transmitted in any form or by any means without prior written permission. No part of this book may be used or reproduced in any manner for the purpose of training artificial intelligence technologies or systems.

All inquiries should be made to the author.

ISBN: 978-1-923225-99-2

A catalogue entry for this book is available from the National Library of Australia.

Project management and text design by Publish Central
Cover design by Julia Kuris

Disclaimer
The material in this publication is of the nature of general comment only and does not represent professional advice. It is not intended to provide specific guidance for particular circumstances, and it should not be relied on as the basis for any decision to take action or not take action on any matter which it covers. Readers should obtain professional advice where appropriate, before making any such decision. To the maximum extent permitted by law, the author and associated entities and publisher disclaim all responsibility and liability to any person, arising directly or indirectly from any person taking or not taking action based on the information in this publication.

Contents

Introduction		1
Stage 1	**CONNECT: Learning experience design**	**19**
Chapter 1	Create personalised, needs-based learning experiences	21
Chapter 2	Set clear expectations of the learning experience	42
Chapter 3	Implement the 'test-teach-test' paradigm	54
Stage 2	**CONSTRUCT: Curriculum development**	**71**
Chapter 4	Create outcomes-based modules of learning	73
Chapter 5	Structure your lessons for success	92
Chapter 6	Systemise, consolidate and leverage your expertise	112
Stage 3	**COMMUNICATE: Resources development and delivery**	**127**
Chapter 7	Choose a user-friendly delivery style that maintains currency	129
Chapter 8	Provide powerful visual learning aids to assist in discovery-based learning	147
Chapter 9	Use techniques to build rapport and maximise engagement	162
Stage 4	**CRITIQUE: Continuous improvement**	**183**
Chapter 10	Provide, request and receive feedback	185
Chapter 11	Process feedback	202
Chapter 12	Implement a reflective practice	213
Conclusion		225
Acknowledgements		228
About the author		229
Endnotes		231

Introduction

Everyone's a teacher?

Yes, everyone is a teacher. Have you taught someone something they didn't know how to do? Then you're a teacher.

Classroom teachers, lecturers, trainers, facilitators, coaches, subject matter experts, parents, siblings, managers, colleagues, bosses, friends, neighbours, even children are all people we can learn from, and all people we can help learn.

The location or participants don't matter, either. Whether you're teaching your grandma how to use her new phone, or your kid how to tie their shoelaces, at home, or in the community, classroom or boardroom, you're involved in the art of transferring knowledge – which is, in essence, what all teaching boils down to.

We can use a lot of different labels for teaching as well, such as lecturing, presenting, facilitating, guiding, coaching, mentoring or training, but they all have one thing in common: knowledge transfer. The person on the other end of that transfer is the learner or the student. The labels are interchangeable, but the core principles remain.

Teaching is at the core of evolution; it's inherent in being human and hardwired into our biology, much like curiosity and learning. It's fundamental to how we've evolved and keep evolving as a species, so you can't really escape it. You really only have two choices: you either learn to become better at it, or you don't.

Regardless of whether teaching comes naturally to you or not, is it a skill you want to improve at? The choice is up to you. If you do want to improve your teaching skills, you've picked up the right book.

Why make the learner central to the learning process?

Tell me and I forget.
Teach me and I remember.
Involve me, and I learn.

Modern variation of ancient Chinese adage

Picture this: I'm in the middle of the Pacific Ocean, on a small coral atoll called Tarawa, the most populated atoll of the island nation of Kiribati. With a population of just over 120,000 in 2010, Kiribati hadn't had significant teacher training since the British occupation ended in the late 1970s. The Australian aid and development project I was involved in was there to change that by helping to upgrade the skills of the lecturers at the local teacher training college.

One of my tasks was to observe classroom practice, give feedback and recommend ideas for improvement in terms of technique and methodology. Most of the techniques being used were those taught in the '70s – 'chalk and talk' style lecturing, requiring learners to regurgitate theory to pass exams. As can be expected from that style of learning, the teacher trainees mostly appeared uninterested and sleepy (if they hadn't already collapsed from the exhaustion of copying copious amounts of notes from the blackboard in the stifling tropical humidity).

'Tell me and I forget.'

During the lecturer training sessions, we did a lot of explaining. We observed teaching practice and gave lots of feedback about how to include student-centred learning activities and create opportunities for discussion. The feedback, however, mostly either fell on deaf ears or was incorporated once or twice before old habits returned.

'Teach me and I remember.'

Deciding that demonstration might be key, I initiated some supplementary classes in which these student-centred games and activities were first demonstrated before being discussed, deconstructed and reconstructed for different learning levels and subject areas. When the teachers could see how new simple ideas could be applied to their own classrooms, pennies started to drop and lesson plans started to improve. As is always the case, some learners take longer than others, but I had one in particular who didn't seem to *want* to grasp the concept of communicative activities and was definitely not including them in his lesson plans. I discussed this with him many times; however, he was determined that his methods were more efficient, and that his students would not respond well to the activities that I was suggesting.

'Involve me, and I learn.'

So I called his bluff. I asked him to create one lesson plan with me based on the communicative approach, using the lesson structure, games and activities we'd been demonstrating and suggesting. After delivering one lesson like that, if he still didn't believe it was the better way, he could go back to doing whatever he liked.

He agreed, reluctantly. To be honest I think he only agreed because he wanted to prove to me I couldn't possibly know what his students really wanted, and these types of techniques really wouldn't work in his classroom. Fair call. I mean, I was an energetic young white woman in the middle of the Pacific telling a tired male senior lecturer how to do the job he'd been doing for more than 20 years.

His next lesson was HILARIOUS.

His lessons were usually very dry, quite monotone and lecture style. In keeping with the 'Maria style' communicative approach he'd been shown, he put on an energetic high-pitched voice – which was very clearly over-enthusiastic and very clearly mocking me. (Mocking is part of the cultural fabric in Kiribati and was warmly welcomed.)

I don't think I've ever had so much fun observing someone teach. The students were a bit confused at first but then threw themselves into it. He played games with them, set up competitive activities and it was *game on*! The students were jostling each other to win, shaking with laughter, yelling out answers and thoroughly enjoying themselves. What a sight to behold!

After the lesson, he came back to the staffroom with his shoulders sagging, shaking his head in disbelief. I smiled and said slowly, 'So, how do you think that went?'

Usually a bit unenthusiastic and resistant, he looked at me with a gleam in his eye and said, 'Maria, you are right. That *was* fun. I've just realised how boring my teaching has been for the last 20 years. I must change this now. It's good. I like it.'

This wasn't a 'flash in the pan' either. To his credit, by the time I left he was close to the top of the list of lecturers for demonstrating best practice in the classroom, and he had also been elevated to a management position within the college.

'Involve me and I learn' – those ancient Chinese philosophers were right. Involve your learners in the learning process by getting them to practise tasks without fear of judgement or punishment, and watch them as they soar. But not all teaching is like that, is it? I've had some phenomenal teachers who have done exactly that, and some abysmal teachers who have done the opposite. Haven't we all?

I've been chastised and belittled, praised and encouraged. I've laughed and listened eagerly, and I've fallen asleep while being lectured to. I've been put on detention for asking questions, and also asked to reteach a concept because the teacher, although incredibly intelligent and kind, could not break it down into language that newbies could understand. I've walked away from some classes, and persevered through others. I've written formal complaints to the college Dean regarding substandard teaching, and also organised heartfelt surprise thankyou gift baskets from incredibly grateful students. I've both failed classes and been awarded subject prizes. I've been pushed in ways that have created unimaginable growth, and in other ways that have stripped me of any confidence I had left. I've handed in projects I worked months on and failed, while for others I've barely tried and passed with flying colours. I've loathed going to class and also genuinely loved it.

What all those experiences have taught me, the good, the bad and the ugly, is that it doesn't really matter what you're learning – whether it's formal or informal, face to face, online or in some kind of blended learning experience – **'real learning' happens when the learner is central to the learning experience, not the teacher.**

Real learning? Yes. Real learning.

What is 'real learning'?

You know those moments when eyes really open. Light-bulb moments click. Loud 'Ahas!' reverberate around the room. Irreversible impact is made. Where all the pieces come together and *thwack*! They get it. They *really* get it.

Real learning is *that* kind of learning.

You've been there, I know you have. Cast your mind back to your favourite teacher – they could have been a teacher in a classroom, or a family member, or anyone who has crossed your path who has given you one of those super positive *Hooley dooley, I'll never forget that* moments. How were they different from other teaching moments? What did that person do differently that makes them unforgettable?

I can almost guarantee you that what they did differently was to put *you* in the centre of the learning experience, not them. The secret bullet for creating learning experiences that change lives is when *you*, the teacher, step out of the drivers' seat and let the learner take the wheel. It may sound counterintuitive but this is what I've learnt, collecting evidence over 40 years in classrooms as a student, teacher, teacher trainer, curriculum developer, instructional designer, vocational training liaison officer, consultant and project manager.

Over these years, I've developed a personal philosophy that revolves around 'teaching' being 'learner centred' – that is, everything revolves around the learner instead of the teacher. This flips the traditional model of teaching on its head. Instead of the teacher at the front, the learners sitting down, listening and regurgitating, the learner is at the front, the teacher sits down and listens, and gets the learner to drive the learning process based on their needs, skills, experience and motivation to be learning in the first place.

Again, counterintuitively, despite cultural differences, the same rules apply wherever you are in the world and whatever demographic you're teaching. I've slowly been collecting evidence of this throughout my teaching and learning journey, which since 1983 has taken me from Australia to Italy, Indonesia, Japan, the United Arab Emirates, the United Kingdom, Samoa, Kiribati, Tuvalu, Hong Kong, Fiji and Norway. I've taught babies, kids, teens and adults right up to their 90s, in community halls in rural areas, inside people's homes, in formal classrooms and in skyscraper conference rooms. Sure, cultural differences and subtle nuances have to be harnessed to be successful in any of those learning spaces, but the same culture of real learning applies wherever you are. Put the learner in the middle of the learning experience, and magic happens. Put the teacher at the front of the classroom and, well, the opposite is likely to happen.

Too many lecturers, teachers and trainers mindlessly rabbit on in half-full rooms, to learners multitasking or engaged in their own whispered conversations. These same lecturers appear shocked when they ask the room for questions and are met with nothing but awkward silence and blank stares. Why? More than likely, the audience weren't really involved in the lecturer's self-centred diatribe, and were instead (bored) witnesses to it. The icing on that proverbial cake is when the lecturer admonishes the audience for 'not paying attention' and gets shirty as the audience goes into 'deer in headlights' mode when asked to give their opinions on the lecture topic. Why would they share an opinion now when this is the first question they've been asked?

Other subject matter experts have overflowing rooms full of eager audience members eating out of the palms of their hands, asking questions, debating key points and signing up for the next class before they've even finished the first.

Why? There's a very simple reason.

The learners are in the centre of the dialogue – involved, intrigued, inspired to be a part of it – not just a passive witness to it.

Why do we need to consider how technology is changing the way we teach?

Changes in technology in the past 20 years have completely changed the way the world operates. If we don't address these changes, we're not going to connect with our learners and how the world 'teaches' today. Traditional methods of teaching and learning have been superseded and if you haven't changed your approach to delivering training in the past five to ten years, you're behind the eight ball.

> Which of these statements do you think are correct? Take a moment to think about this before checking the answers provided.

- The future of work will be less collaborative.
- Changing the modes of delivery (putting training online, for example) is not enough.
- New skills and knowledge can quickly become obsolete in a fast-paced, ever-evolving workplace, and are, therefore, not the ultimate indicators of success.
- Teaching your learners how to think is more important than teaching them skills and knowledge in today's learning and working environments.
- You shouldn't be helping your learners acquire new knowledge and skills.
- The personal growth of your learners is their responsibility.

According to Gallup,[1] here are the statements that need corrections:
- The future of work will be ~~less~~ MORE collaborative.
- You ~~shouldn't~~ SHOULD be helping your learners acquire new knowledge and skills.
- The personal growth of your learners is ~~their~~ YOUR responsibility.

Do you agree?

You don't have to agree, but you can agree that technology has changed the way we live and work. As you'll know if you've spent time with younger generations, they've come through an education system that is based on problem-solving and finding solutions – not just regurgitating knowledge, and they do *not* tolerate being lectured at.

Where do people actually learn?

The well-established theory is that people learn in three different places in a 70:20:10 ratio, as follows:

- **70 = on-the-job learning:** This includes work-related, collaborative, on-the-job performance and support, and getting experience in the real world, learning from professionals in the field or directly in industry.
- **20 = social learning:** This includes learning with peers and colleagues, coaching and mentoring, and any exposure to learning in a non-formal environment.
- **10 = formal learning:** This covers programs, courses or training series delivered by a professional, and any education leading to a skill or qualification.

Surprised? Possibly not if you've heard of 70-20-10 theory before, but what *might* be surprising to you is that the 70-20-10 model is outdated now thanks to the changes technology has been making.

According to a Training Industry report from 2018,[2] the 70-20-10 model had already changed dramatically for employees and executives. In short:

- On-the-job learning had decreased (to 55 per cent) because employers were offering more formal learning opportunities as part of employment benefits.
- The role of social learning had increased (to 25 per cent) due to shifts in technology.
- Formal learning had increased (to 20 per cent).

With the advent of artificial intelligence (AI), can you imagine how drastically those figures are going to change again in the next five to ten years? Here's a question for you to ponder.

> 💡 How do global changes affect the way you teach, coach or train your learners? What changes could you consider making to the way you deliver?

Why are you here?

Whether you're a subject-matter expert delivering your own learning experiences, or you're working in a position that oversees learning, training or education in an organisation, picking up a book like this tells me you're the kind of person who cares.

You're here because you *don't* want to be a belligerent 'I am the master!' lecturer type of character; you'd much prefer to be a renowned, admired and respected thought leader who automatically creates lifelong referees out of loyal learners. Or perhaps you know deep down that 'tick and flick' learning simply doesn't work, and you want those learning in your organisation not to be wasting time, effort or funds participating in training that isn't going to produce a return on investment.

You're someone who cares deeply enough about your field and the people who are learning from you that you will invest in whatever it takes to make your learning experiences exemplary. Beige is not good enough – never has been, never will be.

Neither you nor your organisation is a generic, ubiquitous, 'supermarket' brand; you're the unique five-star boutique version. Nothing else is like you on the market and you've worked a lifetime to build your reputation based on doing the hard yards out there in the field. It stands to reason, then, that your learning resources need to match that reputation – you don't see the Ritz Carlton providing 'supermarket brand' refreshments, so why would you risk your reputation by providing substandard learning experiences?

You're here because you know your knowledge makes a difference in the world and when people apply it, they can change their lives in extraordinary ways – you know extraordinary change happens when learners have the chance to be involved in extraordinary, transformational learning experiences. This is what this book will do – help extraordinary people like you create extraordinary learning resources that create real change in the world and confirm you as the five-star professional you are.

Now just to further qualify whether you're reading the right book or not, this book is for you if:

- You have lots of learning content ready, and you know it needs a revamp.
- When you deliver content in a face-to-face setting, you're not convinced you're doing everything possible to make it as 'punchy' as it can be.
- Your courses aren't getting the engagement or results you'd like.
- You have lots more content lurking in your archives, hard drives (or still stuck in your head!) that you know you need to develop.
- You don't have enough time or know-how to put your content together in a way that will have the impact you know it's capable of having (online or in a face-to-face setting).
- You're feeling a bit disorganised, or in procrasti-something mode when it comes to tackling this project. (There's always a more important KPI, or cleaning, gardening or cooking to do, so it keeps going on the back-burner.)
- You know you can do it, but just need a framework to work within. You're good at following instructions if you have the right direction.

This book is not for you if:

- You're a killer presenter who can engage an audience from 'go to whoa', in online, face-to-face or self-study scenarios.
- You've got an awesome team of VAs, designers and producers, and internationally qualified, culturally aware instructional designers ready to create best practice resources for you.
- You just need to create compliance-based 'tick and flick' learning – for knowledge that you know the learner will not retain or be able to apply in the field.

So why would you want to learn about teaching and learning from me?

Good question. Who am I to talk about teaching and learning? Well, I'm not a tech-expert or HR person who fell into learning and development by accident. I've been an avid learner since the age of three – when my six-year-old brother came home with homework and I was more interested in completing it than he was. I've always been an avid reader and have won scholarships to study abroad twice – once in high school and once at university. I've studied six languages and have accumulated more qualifications than I can poke a stick at. I've been teaching, developing curriculum and training teachers internationally for more than 25 years and can hand on heart guarantee you that what I've learnt in a classroom and from living and learning all over the world has far outweighed anything I've ever learnt as part of a qualification.

My real teaching qualifications have come from having had 18 overseas postings and having worked (and been a learner) at all levels of education and training: primary, secondary, vocational, corporate, tertiary and postgraduate. I've worked with subject matter experts in fields as diverse as accounting to neuroscience and, as a believer in lifelong learning, I'm always enrolled in some kind of course – be it another master's degree, a women's health course or cooking class. I'm constantly looking for better ways to teach and learn, and am proud to call myself a bona fide 'ednerd', through and through. At your service!

Seeing extraordinary individuals who are passionate about their field become extraordinary teachers absolutely lights me up and gets a fire going in my belly, as does completely reinventing a department or organisation, and the way they deliver education and training. Seeing lacklustre slide decks and workbooks develop into catalysts for real, life-changing learning experiences literally brings tears to my eyes (ask any of my clients who have nailed their learning resources); I wear my heart on my sleeve and when something rocks, you'll know about it.

That feeling is the reason I am writing this book. These skills are not hard to learn, and they're easy to implement. Knowing how to create extraordinary learning experiences out of your knowledge and expertise is not something that AI can do for you (just yet in a face-to-face environment at least!), but it's also not rocket science either.

I wholeheartedly believe that quality education should be a birthright, and that is why I invite you on a learning journey that will hopefully change the way you think about how education works, forever.

How is this book different from other teaching and learning books?

To answer that question, check out the following table.

How this book is different from other learning resources

What this book's not	What this book is
All theory, no practical action	All demonstration, lots of practical and actionable tips, tricks and strategies
Research-based	Evidence-based
Peer-reviewed	Classroom-tested
Academic-level concepts and language	Everyday conversations about practical strategies and techniques
'Print and use' lesson plans	Reflective and implementation-based tasks
Targeted at either children or adults	Applicable to intergenerational learning and teaching
Single approach or principle with rigorous academic detail	International, multi-disciplinary perspective on a wide range of learning theories, principles, philosophies, strategies and techniques
Targeting only face-to-face interaction or online learning	Applicable to any learning environment

So, in essence, this book is for anyone who is responsible for teaching and learning – whether you're teaching your colleagues about insider trading or a bunch of carpenters how to install plasterboard, and whether you're a subject-matter expert in a specific field or responsible for learning and development pathways in your organisation.

Whoever, whatever, wherever, however you're teaching, while reading this book I ask you to think deeply. Consider your own context while we have a long, reflective conversation about teaching and learning at any age or in any industry, in any learning environment. Think about what works and doesn't work when it comes to motivating your learners, keeping them engaged, and helping them kick serious learning and development goals.

How can you get the most out of this book?

This book takes you on a journey through what I believe are the four stages to creating extraordinary learning experiences: *connect*, *construct*, *communicate* and *critique*. Each of these stages contains three chapters.

Depending on where you're at with your content, curriculum and resources development, you may be able to skim over some of the stages. Having said that, 'every day's a school day', right? Every chapter is full of funny (or inspiring or downright tear-jerker) anecdotes I've collected from living, learning, teaching and working all over the globe. If you like to have a laugh and big 'Aha!' light-bulb style moments while you're learning, I'd urge you to get a cuppa and make a weekend out of it – and also grab something to take notes on, because every chapter has practical tasks and reflections to get you thinking about your own learning content and how you can improve it.

If you don't like to have fun, think deeply and take practical action immediately, I suggest you close this book now and pass it along to someone who does.

Right. Brilliant. You're still here. So, what's the best way to work out which parts of the book you need to engage with?

First of all, I simply had too much content for one book, so I've created a space where you'll find a lot of extra material: the Resources page of my website. Scan the provided QR code and you'll be taken to this page. You can also access the page via mariadoyle.com/everyones-a-teacher-resources/.

In the introductions to each of the four stages on the Resources page, you'll find a link to a diagnostic tool for the three chapters within each stage. Using this diagnostic tool will help you assess your current knowledge and skills, so you can focus on the chapters that you need the most.

An important part of motivating learners to engage in learning is helping them decide whether they really want or need the content you're about to teach them. This book is all about demonstrating best practice, so in the first three chapters of the book, I've also included a 'pre-test' section, which reiterates what's in the online diagnostic for all chapters. This is so that whether you're using the online diagnostic or not, you'll experience how powerful the 'pre-testing' concept can be at least in the first three chapters. Chapter 3 is dedicated to unravelling the psychology behind this concept, which is why the first three chapters are designed this way – to give you a real-life demonstration.

The pre-tests (online diagnostics) contain two parts: skills and knowledge checks.

What's the purpose of the skills check?
The skills check asks you to rate yourself against the skills discussed in that chapter. If you're not doing all of these things or are unsure as to why you would need to, I recommend reading that chapter in full.

What's the purpose of the knowledge check?
The knowledge check is a series of statements that may or may not be true, based on the topic of that chapter. If you can't say which of those statements are true with confidence (and explain why), you may also benefit from reading the whole chapter.

If you do get perfect 'scores' for any of the chapters, there's no harm in skimming through the chapter to confirm that you're on the right track – you'll also get some international teaching and learning stories to read along the way! Whatever your approach, I'd recommend starting at the beginning and working through the chapters chronologically, because they do build on each other.

Through the book, you'll also find a few references to *The Engagement ToolKit: A Facilitator's Guide to Breaking the Lecture Habit*, also available via my Resources page. This is a collection of activities I use in my classrooms, both online and face to face, which put the learner in the centre of the classroom and create a collaborative, communicative learning environment. It's a separate resource because I simply don't have enough space to squeeze all those activities into the one book! But it will always be freely available via my website, so take advantage of it whenever you need some inspiration or a quick refresher on ways to engage your learners.

What's my promise?

If you're still here, it's because something is resonating with you. Perhaps:

- You know you can do better when it comes to your learning materials.
- You have *no* desire to be that uninspiring lecturer type.
- You truly want to create extraordinary experiences packed full of 'real learning' that will create real change in the worlds of your learners.

Whatever the reason, my promise is that if you read this book and learn nothing, I will not only offer you a full refund, but also video myself while standing on my head proclaiming loudly I'm a dumb-dumb and post it all over socials.

Okay, that's a lie; I don't know how to stand on my head but I *do* know that this book is full of 'Aha!' moments. I've literally dumped over 30 years of teaching and learning lessons into the next few hundred pages – so sit back, enjoy the process, be immersed in the strategies and, above all, have a go at the activities and reflections at the end of each chapter. These activities are where the magic happens!

> **Remember: you are extraordinary. What you teach is extraordinary and has the potential to change lives.**

By following the suggestions in this book, you too can create extraordinary learning experiences that confirm you (and your organisation) as the expert in your niche – who everyone recommends as the one to work with if you really want to excel in a certain field.

So, strap in! You're in for a wild ride that will take you on a teaching and learning journey around the world – including stories about a mute Japanese child who started to speak, Afghani interpreters who stormed out of my classroom disgusted, a grandmother in the Pacific who told me I had a large backside, Norwegian lecturers who didn't believe in marking criteria, and a shy young Australian scientist who transformed right before our very eyes into confident, fun-loving, vocal young man, due to a simple technique that I'll also teach you how to use.

Ready to learn?
Grab a notebook and a pen if you're old-school like me.
Prefer digital? Open a notes application on your device.
Let's go!

OUTCOME: Design a learning experience that caters to the needs of your learners

STAGE 1

CONNECT: Learning experience design

Many people think the key to improving a learning experience is 'fixing' their slide decks or worksheets. Before you even consider your learning resources, however, you need to ensure that the experience is designed to suit the needs of the intended learners. This is why the key word here is *connect*: getting to know your learners as individuals, why they're working with you, what they're hoping to achieve and setting clear expectations so you're all on the same page – before you start working together.

Creating a safe, trusted, connected learning environment is essential to keeping your learners engaged; this 'safe' space is where learners are confident to explore, learn, grow, and 'have a go' without fear of humiliation, punishment or 'doing it alone'. When you get the foundations right, learners *want* to attend classes because they know they're going to get a personalised learning experience that is tailored to what they need, and the way they learn best – and that creates an awesome atmosphere that most learners are keen to be part of.

It's also about working *with* the mix of learners you're bound to have in your classrooms. When you consider the mix of generations, cultures and professions you may have in front of you, connecting is about helping you and them work together to get the best out of each other, and to collaborate and thrive as a collective.

What happens when you don't *connect* with your learners properly?

You risk 'losing' your students or barely being able to engage them. Attendance might drop, engagement may be low, the atmosphere in your classes may be lacklustre or, at worst, antagonistic. Learners may feel disengaged, bored or alienated from the lessons, their peers or their facilitator. No-one wants to be a learner in a classroom where they feel left out, ostracised or disengaged because they're being taught what they already know, don't need or aren't in any way motivated by.

Consider teaching how to cook rice, for example. You'd approach it differently with 12-year-old kids going camping, than you would with senior chefs in training for Michelin-Star restaurants. Those two groups have completely different motivations for learning, they're from different generations, and they're going to use that skill in very different circumstances; therefore, even though the theory of rice + water + heat will be similar, the how, when and where (and even if) you teach that skill needs to be different if it's going to 'land' for both of those groups.

This is by far the most important stage in creating extraordinary learning experiences, and that's why it's up first (and far more complex than the other stages). If you don't get this stage right, the state of your curriculum and learning resources are literally meaningless.

What type of learning experience do you want to design? One that falls flat and frustrates your learners? Or one that has your learners engaged, kicking goals and telling everyone how good it was to learn with you?

If you really want to *connect* with your learners, you'll need to:
- create personalised, needs-based learning experiences
- set clear expectations of the learning experience
- implement the test-teach-test paradigm.

These coincidentally are the topics for the first three chapters of this book.

If you're pretty sure you've got this stage covered already, confirm it by doing the stage 1 diagnostic on the Resources page on the website – scan the QR code to access.

If you do 'score' highly, I'd still recommend skimming through the chapters, just to confirm you're not missing anything.

CHAPTER 1

Create personalised, needs-based learning experiences

The outcome

Create personalised, needs-based learning experiences

The why

Why do we need to create personalised, needs-based training solutions?

Because, quite simply, no two learners are the same.

When you don't create personalised, needs-based training solutions, you're unlikely to connect properly with your learners. You could be pitching above or below their level, trying to teach them things they already know, making the learning experience unnecessarily difficult for them, or completely alienating them by ignoring the reason they're working with you in the first place. You could, if you don't know enough about their cultural or social background, also be unknowingly insulting them.

Don't learn the hard way, like I did.

I was teaching a class of beginner English students at a suburban vocational college in Australia. Most of the learners were adult immigrants and refugees, and we were talking about their home culture and what their home towns looked like (using basic language to describe the landscape and townscape). One of the girls, who was usually quite chatty, was silent for the whole lesson, regardless of the prompts I gave her. Thinking she was just having an off day, I let her be.

At the end of the class, she came up to me, nudged me, and said, 'I'm sorry, I don't know my home country. I was born in a refugee camp – I live there my whole life. I don't want to talk about refugee camps as my home country. I must?'

No words can really describe how incredibly stupid, ashamed and ignorant I felt at that moment.

> 'To assume makes an ASS out of U and ME.'

Indeed, it does. I was lucky this student was brave enough to confront me about it. Many students wouldn't be in that situation. As a young, clueless English teacher, I hadn't taken the time to get to know her and her background, and it created an incredibly humiliating experience for both her and me.

So what's the solution?

It's pretty simple. You ask questions. Generally speaking, you ask your learners about four broad areas *before* you start working with them:
1. their educational, industry and field experience
2. their personal goals
3. any barriers to learning they may have
4. their learning styles.

If there are wider learning and development goals that need to align with organisational or industry requirements, these also need to be taken into consideration.

Core concepts 'pre-test' – do you really need this chapter?

If you've already done the stage 1 diagnostic, you can skip over the skills and knowledge checks and start at the 'The "what, when and how" (the theory)' section. If you haven't done the online diagnostic, answer the following questions.

CHAPTER 1: Create personalised, needs-based learning experiences ■ 23

SKILLS CHECK: How much are you already doing?
- Getting to know your learners by asking them before you start teaching them about their educational, industry and field experience, their personal goals, any barriers to learning they may have, and their learning styles.
- If working in a group environment, creating 'getting to know you activities' so learners can learn more about each other.
- Mixing up the types of activities that you do when teaching, to cater for a variety of different generations, learning needs and learning styles.
- Changing the way you teach depending on which learners present to you at any given time.
- Prioritising creating a safe, trusted environment over all else in the learning spaces you're the facilitator for.

KNOWLEDGE CHECK: Which of the following statements do you think are true? Can you explain the reasons for your choices?
1. Finding out more about your learners' personal goals and barriers to learning helps create a safe and trusted learning environment, but isn't really possible when you're working with large groups, especially when they're online.
2. Barriers to learning could involve religious or cultural restrictions that make it difficult for your learners to attend classes or do homework tasks; as the facilitator, it's best that you know about these things so that you can cater for them if possible.
3. You are most likely dominant in one 'learning style' and one 'intelligence' across most activities and tasks.
4. Detailers need to see the big picture before they can process the details of the learning content.
5. The aim of universal design is not to cater for every type of learner in every activity, but to ensure that all types of learning styles and intelligences are catered for, to some extent, throughout the learning experience to ensure equity.

If you're unsure about using the skills listed, or are not confident explaining why the knowledge check statements are true or false, this chapter is for you!*

The 'what, when and how' (the theory)

In this chapter, we're going to discuss what questions to ask, and when and how to ask them, so that you can create a safe, trusted learning environment for your learners. Please note that I won't be going deeper into how to conduct training needs analyses that align with organisational needs and industry requirements – that's a whole other book!

What kinds of questions might you ask?

A lot of suggested areas to ask questions about are included here, and obviously not all learning situations require you to cover all of them. For now, keep an open mind and imagine a teaching situation where you're transferring knowledge to learners.

> 💡 **Consider why you would want to ask questions in the areas provided** – what could they possibly help you understand (or avoid)? The rationale for asking questions like these will follow.

Potential areas to ask questions about include:
- **Educational or industry background:**
    - existing or partially completed qualifications
    - where they've worked and for how long
    - whether they've ever taken a course or been informally trained in the course subject matter before.

---

*   Knowledge check answers: Statements 2 and 5 are correct. The others are not correct. You'll find out why during the chapter!

- **Personal goals:**
    - their 'why' for studying – what motivates them to come to your classes
    - their career or personal aspirations
    - where they hope to see themselves in the future.
- **Barriers to learning:**
    - **Family needs:** curfews, childcare or other family care needs.
    - **Learning challenges:**
        - cognitive (such as dyslexia, ADHD, anxiety or depression)
        - physical (for example, poor eyesight or hearing, migraine sufferer, diabetic, heart issues)
        - linguistic (for example, having English as an additional language).
    - **Religious or cultural restrictions:**
        - gender-based (such as not being able to work alone with a colleague of the opposite sex)
        - topic-based (for example, Jehovah's Witnesses not being allowed to discuss or celebrate Christmas, Easter or birthdays)
        - celebration-based (for example, Muslims needing to fast during daylight hours in Ramadan)
        - food- and drink-based (for example, how some religions prohibit the consumption of pork or alcohol).
    - **History of trauma:** consider whether your learners have a history that includes immigration, refugee status, and/or PTSD from a traumatic event such as the loss of their home, the death of a family member, a house fire, war, an accident or emergency situation. Trauma can last a lifetime and learners can turn up with any degree of resolved or unresolved trauma in their distant or recent past.
- **Learning styles:**
    - Group versus one to one – do they prefer to work alone or in a group?
    - Visual, audio or kinaesthetic – do they prefer to learn by watching, listening or doing?
    - Generational – which generation do they identify with?

What are the benefits of asking questions like these?

Good question! Remember, not all questions are feasible to ask in all situations, but considering the learning environment you find yourself in, the answers may save you unnecessary embarrassment or challenging situations when you're teaching.

Let's start with their educational or industry background

If you know what your learners have already been trained in, you can avoid teaching them what they already know. If they have zero background knowledge or training in your area, you know you're starting with a clean slate – but this does tend to be quite rare in most teaching and learning contexts with adults.

Some teachers may consider it challenging to have learners who think they 'know it all' already, but I prefer to flip that thinking. Think of them as free, extra 'experts' or human resources who can help take the load off you as the only teacher. They can help you out when other learners ask tricky questions, for example, if you open the question up to the whole group. You could redirect like this:

> 'Well, that's a great question! We have some very experienced people in this room who may like to help answer that question! Bob! What's your experience in this case? What would you do?'

#handball ... No but seriously, learners having prior knowledge, training and experience can be of great service to you in a classroom if you learn to harness it and use it to your advantage. And you never know, you might learn something yourself! At a bare minimum, you might find gaps in their knowledge or different ways of doing things, which are all great fodder for classroom discussion and group learning opportunities.

If you're working with large groups, you can also use the more experienced people in the group as 'group leaders' and split the class into several smaller groups to discuss scenarios, practical tasks or problem-solving activities.

Using these strategies helps create a collaborative, communicative, group approach to learning rather than an old-school, 'I'm the teacher listen to me' lecture-style experience. Which would you prefer to be involved in as a teacher and a learner?

Why is knowing personal goals important for you as the teacher?

It's the difference between helping a teen who wants to bake a cake to impress their mum on their birthday, and helping another teen who is obsessed with baking and wants to open a patisserie some day. Their motivations are different, and therefore their attention to detail, their depth of understanding and their ability to remember steps or how and why to do things certain ways will be completely different. So the way you teach them will need to be completely different too.

Think about why your learners are in front of you – are they honestly interested in learning lifelong skills they see themselves using in years to come? Or is it more of a bucket list item they're trying to tick off? Or a new hobby or interest they're exploring to see if they'd like to pursue it more seriously? Or are they simply there for compliance reasons?

If you know their motivations for learning, and how important that learning is for their future, you'll know exactly how much energy they're going to bring to the learning experience, and how much energy, time and commitment to match to theirs.

We've all taught people who simply are *not* interested in the subject matter – it's like pulling teeth, isn't it? The only thing worse than not realising that is pouring your heart and soul into trying to help someone who really couldn't care less either way. Save your time and energy for those who will appreciate it – and trim back the learning experience for those who won't. The former bunch will thank you for it, and the latter bunch will too.

Knowing their motivations and personal goals will also help you help them be realistic about what they're going to achieve while working with you. That teen who wants to learn how to bake for a living – if they really do want to become a Michelin-Star level pastry chef, they'll need to be realistic about how much time and effort they're going to have to put into learning about basic ingredients and flavour profiles, equipment and cooking-related chemistry. That teen who just wants to bake their mum a cake for her birthday will likely be happy to settle for a spatula and a packet cake mix – teaching the ins and outs of baking chemistry to a kid who just wants to do something nice for his mum is pointless!

Understanding their end goals, and working with them to achieve them at the intensity they want and need, helps build trust and rapport with your learners – regardless of their age, motivations for learning or experience in the field.

How does knowing about barriers to learning help you as the teacher, and also help the learner?

Regardless of whether the barriers to learning are due to family, physical, cognitive, linguistic, cultural or trauma reasons, knowing about them is going to help you create a safer learning environment for everyone involved. Give them a chance to be open and honest about the reasons they may not be able to come to class, or participate fully. Knowing the 'why' will help you create an environment where they can participate as fully as possible.

This also saves the embarrassment of being presented with a barrier in the middle of a class and being blindsided by it, like I was in my story about the student who had only ever lived in a refugee camp. Cultural barriers aren't always easy to foresee either, especially if you're clueless about cultures other than your own. This is how I was when I was very new to teaching, and working in a vocational college with a group of Afghani interpreters who had been working for the Australian government before being relocated to Australia for their own safety. I had no idea of their backgrounds until we had a classroom discussion about household chores; one of the European class members started discussing how men in Europe were happy to clean toilets and vacuum floors, and that if the guys wanted a wife in Australia they would need to learn how to do these things. An all-out argument soon erupted in the middle of my classroom – and, being young and having had no exposure to Middle Eastern culture, I had literally no concept of what could possibly have been offensive or created such division between the classmates. We all had a cultural lesson that day.

Another story that springs to mind is when I was asked to train a large number of vocational college lecturers who were getting consistently poor reviews from their international students. As this was considered a business risk for the college, I was brought in to tackle the problem. I wondered whether the problem was actually based on a lack of international cultural understanding, and to figure this out I created a short quiz on the flags, national dishes and what is considered 'rude' behaviour in the top 25 nationalities of learners who attended that college. Unsurprisingly, most of them knew very little about the nationalities they were teaching.

Learning about the backgrounds and cultures of your learners if you're in a multicultural environment is crucial if your aim is to remove barriers like cultural misunderstandings between them, yourself and all the learners in that learning space.

Likewise, if you know a learner has a cognitive or physical challenge that makes sitting in a classroom difficult, if you have capacity you can make allowances so that the learner has the best possible chance of participation. I had a Brazilian learner once who was so fidgety he couldn't sit through a day in a classroom. He explained his condition and, working with the college, we came up with some adjustments for him – including allowing him to pace or stand, and take notes at the back of the classroom instead of using a chair. I also incorporated many more group discussion activities that could be done standing up. The change was positive for all classroom members – they didn't have a restless classmate anymore, and they got a lot more time moving around, which really kept the energy in the classroom high.

Don't think of having to deal with learning barriers as something that needs to be tedious or difficult. See it as an opportunity to get to know your learners better, and help them get the most out of your learning experience. Sometimes making adjustments for barriers can actually advantage everyone involved – like in the case of that Brazilian learner.

Also keep in mind that learning difficulties can stem from a number of factors, including conditions such as dyslexia, dyspraxia, dysgraphia, auditory or visual processing disorders, ADHD or even geographical factors such as having English as an additional language. Issues such as shyness or an unwillingness to participate could also be connected to gender identity, past trauma, previous unsavoury learning experiences or neurodivergence.

If you've never heard of these potential barriers to learning, and wish to learn more about how they may affect your learners, be proactive: do a quick online search and read up on them. Learners may not even be aware of what barriers to learning they have, but if you're experiencing issues with your learners it's always a good idea to think a bit deeper about what could actually be going on beneath the surface. Be curious – imagine how differently that lesson could have gone for the refugee student if I had dug a little deeper! (We explore this concept much more in the final stage of this book: *critique*.)

A final story to really bring this point home is the story of a young girl I taught English to when I was working in Japan. During the handover, I was told she was simply impossible to manage in the classroom on account of her throwing tantrums and destroying activities at every opportunity. The advice from the teacher handing over to me was that she was best off being manhandled into the 'naughty corner' and then left there for the entirety of the lesson. During our first lesson, the young girl did exactly what the teachers had said she would do. The lesson was reduced to absolute chaos. Instead of getting angry, however, and using the 'naughty corner', I tried a different approach: simply shutting down games once they were destroyed with silence and comments like, 'Oh well, let's do some quiet activities now'.

Over time, she started to try to participate in games by lining up and being part of the team. Although she didn't answer questions or 'win' any points, she was at least being part of the activities as best she could. One day, she actually answered a question (albeit incorrectly) and I realised I had never before heard her say a word – in Japanese or English – rather just screaming or grunting or crying. I reported back to the other teachers, who were as gobsmacked as I was. Months later, when I was leaving Japan, the parents of this child approached me in tears, begging me to stay and live with their family as a private tutor for their daughter. They promised me a generous salary and free accommodation but I had plans to return to Australia so explained I couldn't take the position. In a last-ditch effort to get me to stay, they explained that before my classes their daughter had been completely non-verbal in any language, including Japanese – and that since I had started teaching her, she had started to speak.

The girl was eight years old. I'm not crying, you're crying (actually, we were all crying by that point).

The moral of the story? Barriers to learning are about as common as learners who don't really want to be there – they're everywhere, and avoiding them isn't going to make them go away. The more you ignore them, the more the barriers will impact your learning spaces and the less you will connect with all your learners.

Be open, be curious, be kind – it takes all types!

Do you really need to cater for all learning styles?

The short answer to that, is no. That's like saying you can cater for all tastes and flavour profiles in a single restaurant. Variety is good, but covering all bases is near impossible. It's about knowing enough about your learners to:

- avoid making the learning experience unnecessarily harder for them
- choose activities that you know they'll enjoy participating in.

You've likely heard of visual, audio and kinaesthetic (or tactile) learners, but do you know how to cater for them in your classroom?

> **To find out what you already know about catering for different learning styles, give the following quiz a go. Decide on the statements you think are true – the answers are provided after the statements.**

1. Kinaesthetic (or tactile) learners need more breaks when studying or reading.
2. It's a good idea to suggest to kinaesthetic (or tactile) learners that walking, rocking or moving while reading or studying may help them learn better.
3. Visual learners are not likely to be distracted by sounds.
4. Writing things down helps visual learners.

5. Auditory learners will benefit less from having a discussion about something, and more from trying out the activity for themselves.
6. An auditory learner may hum or talk to themselves while listening to you, which makes it seem like they're not paying attention (but they probably are, and are digesting everything you're saying).
7. Generalists need to see the big picture before they can understand the details, whereas detailers have no need to see the big picture.

Only two of these statements are not true – statements three and five. Do you know why? Visual learners *can* be distracted by sounds (and speaking from experience as a predominantly visual learner, I *cannot* focus if music or repetitive noises are in the background), and auditory learners will benefit *more* from having discussions. Tactile learners benefit more from having a go at the activity themselves.

Many more learning styles exist than just these three, though – have you heard of multiple intelligences, for example? As explained in various academic papers and available in simple form at LiteracyNet.org,[3] you and your learners might identify with other learning styles. Do any of these sound like you, or someone you know?

- **Spatial intelligence:** Likes to think in 3D and is engaged with colour coding, charts, posters and mind maps.
- **Logic or math intelligence:** Likes organising and abstract thinking, and is engaged with critical thinking activities.
- **Musical intelligence:** Sensitive to rhythm, pitch and intonation, can remember tunes and rhythms easily and likes musically guided imagery.
- **Naturalist intelligence:** Sensitive to nature and environment, likes to work and walk outside and in nature, likes studying about nature, animals, the outdoors.
- **Social or interpersonal intelligence:** Likes interacting with people, is sensitive to others and likes problem-solving verbally.
- **Self or intrapersonal intelligence:** Is aware of their feelings and is engaged by reflective or storytelling activities.

Imagine trying to engage a spatial learner by talking about their feelings, or an intrapersonal learner with abstract problems? It would be far less productive than giving the spatial learners a mind-mapping exercise and the intrapersonal learners the opportunity to share stories, right?

> 💡 **Here's another spanner we can throw into the proverbial works – are you usually dominant in only one learning style? Go back to the lists provided, and think about yourself and how you learn.**

Are people usually dominant in only one 'learning style' and one 'intelligence'? The answer is ... NO! Really? Yes, really. People can be dominant in different styles and intelligences in general, but usually it depends on the activity. Take me, for example:

- **The visual learner:** When it comes to getting directions, show me a map and I have a near photographic memory. Explain it to me? I'm lost. I learn by seeing the map, and having it imprinted into my memory.
- **The audio learner:** I failed history at school. We had to memorise dates and events from a book and I couldn't remember any of it. If someone tells it to me as a story, though, I'll be able to recount it. (And probably add a few embellishments and hand gestures to spice it up – I can't help it, I have Irish blood and I'm half Italian.) I learn by hearing the story, visualising the plot and characters, and remembering the person and how they told it. So that's where my visual and audio styles come together to work alongside each other.
- **The kinaesthetic learner:** Cooking? Recipe books? No way. Inspiration maybe, but just give me the ingredients and let me experiment. Hand me the knife, let me chop, sauté and taste till I'm happy with it. I learn by doing it myself, and making mistakes and adjustments until I get it right. This is why I can't bake cakes to save my life. Following instructions that require chemical accuracy? Nahhhhh. Making it up as I go along, tasting and testing until it's right? Yep. That's me.

So why have I just spent the last few thousand words banging on about learning styles and intelligences then? Is catering to different learning styles redundant? No, not really. People have a variety of different learning styles, so it's best practice to mix up the way you teach so that different types of learners can benefit from different activities.

And we haven't even covered why knowing which generation someone identifies with is crucial in being able to 'reach' them in a classroom. Can you imagine trying to teach an 80-year-old the way you'd teach a 14-year-old? Or why you might have problems with classroom dynamics if you've got boomers, who were born between 1946 and 1964, trying to work on projects with millennials, who were born nearly half a century later?

Boomers are accustomed to lectures, millennials are not. Attention spans of younger generations are getting shorter with the increasing prevalence of working online, social media and instant gratification. Having said that, because they're considered 'digital natives', their sleuthing skills when it comes to finding answers on the net may be far more advanced than those of boomers (who due to their age and exposure to using the internet, may not have a well-developed skillset in that area).

This is not to say that different generations *can't* work together, but their skill sets and expectations of the learning environment will be different – and this is a fantastic learning opportunity for a new group of learners to learn more about each other and how they can work better together as a team.

If you have classrooms with various generations, what a great way to open a class by looking at the different ways they're accustomed to learning, and pointing out the strengths that each generation presents with. Not only will it help them understand each other's needs, but they can also support each other in group learning tasks by taking on the tasks they know they're best suited for in group activities – isn't that a skill that would be helpful in any working environment?

How do you cater for all these learning styles in one classroom, or encourage learners to reflect on their own learning styles?

As Yale's Poorvu Center for Teaching and Learning points out, 'over 71 separate learning-style instruments and theories have been documented in education literature', and 'a broader approach that invites students to reflect on their learning, rather than narrow their style down, has been shown to improve learning outcomes.'[4]

Again, catering for all learning styles is a bit like trying to cater for all the flavour profiles in a single restaurant. You can't really. You can do one of two things:

1. cater for as many as possible within reason
2. go niche and cater for a restricted number that suits the profiles of the people you have in front of you at the time.

It's very similar in a classroom. If you're teaching something super niche to a niched group of individuals – such as how to service a motorbike to a small bunch of teenagers – you'll likely have success with some visual demonstrations, some TikTok video disaster reels, some short sharp storytelling and some practical activities so they can give it a go with guidance. If you're teaching the same skillset to a community class with teenagers right through to retirees, you may need to reconsider your approach.

You can't cater for all learning styles at all times, but you can mix it up so you're appealing to as many styles as possible. In other words, you don't need to think about creating an activity specifically to cater for visual learners only, or be worried that visual learners won't 'get it' if you create an activity that suits audio learners better. Creating a variety of activities that cater for different styles throughout the lesson is key.

Remember, many different ways to learn are possible, and no-one fits into any one box. Every learner will present unique learning challenges, and it's best to get them involved in understanding their own learning styles so they can identify the types of activities they enjoy (or adapt them to suit themselves). It's also helpful in terms of knowing which learning products to offer (online, face to face, audio-based podcasts, video tutorials or blended learning options).

If you're keen to find out which styles you're dominant in, or you wish to survey your own learners, a raft of surveys is available online.[5]

You may also benefit from understanding the difference between right and left brain dominance, which indicates whether you're more analytical and methodical (left-brained) or more creative and artistic (right-brained). This may make a big difference to the way you deliver information – for example, if you're pitching to a bunch of artists versus a room of accountants. According to research from Veena Deshmukh and colleagues (shown in the following figure), creatives are most likely to be auditory dominant learners.[6] Does that surprise you? (It surprised me – I thought creatives would be visually dominant).

Left-brain dominant learning style (analytical and methodical) versus right-brain dominant learning style (creative and artistic)

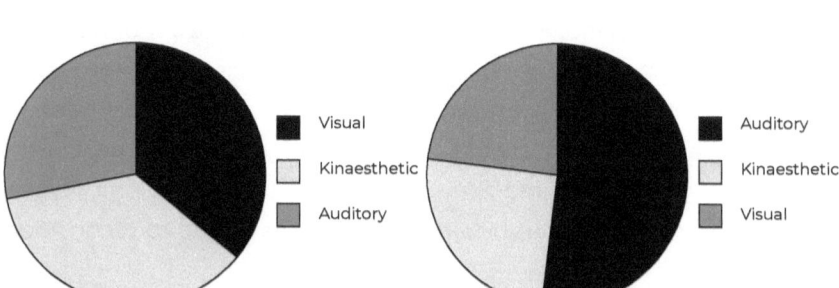

> 💡 Do you teach a certain niche of people? Does this make you want to do some research into what styles they may be dominant in?

Demonstrate with clear examples

> ### What type of activities appeal to different types of learners?
>
> If the key is 'mixing it up' for a large group of learners, here are some examples of the different types of activities that would appeal to different learning styles:
> - **Visual:** A labelled graphic, diagrams, video explainers.
> - **Tactile:** A practical, hands-on task, either alone or in groups.
> - **Audio:** Live interviews, lectures, storytelling and music.
> - **Generalist:** Providing an overview outline, or broad outcome statements.
> - **Detailer:** Providing many examples to demonstrate a point, and scenario-based questions.
> - **Spatial:** Providing or getting the learner to create visual stories, posters or charts.
> - **Logic/maths:** Using puzzles, and drag-and-drop, mix-and-match activities.
> - **Social/interpersonal:** Group problem-solving discussion.
> - **Self/intrapersonal:** Reflective writing activities.
> - **Macro skills:** Mix them up!

Although not strictly speaking a 'learning style', the four core macro skills of language are also important to consider when thinking about creating a variety of activities for your learners.

Macro what? Macro skills: the four ways we use language to learn, which are reading, writing (written language), listening and speaking (oral language, which includes sign language). While an audio learner might really enjoy a one-hour lecture, others may not. This is why it's beneficial to mix up the activities during a lesson. Instead of lecturing for an hour straight, try the following process:
- listening to some core content
- discussing it with their peers
- reading some more core content
- writing about it.

This way, learners are engaging all four of the macro skills, and lessons won't only seem to go faster, they'll also be far more interactive and engaging. We'll go deeper into the macro skills concept in the third section of this book, when we explore creating and delivering engaging learning resources.

When and how do you ask learners about their needs?

Remember – a difference exists between *you* understanding what your learners need as a learner, and *your learners* getting to know each other if they're learning in a group situation. You need to get your learners opening up and sharing about themselves so they can enjoy the most productive learning environment possible. You can do this in two ways:

1. **Pre-course survey:** This will give you the information *you* need to adapt the course to their needs (and would normally be considered private and confidential).
2. **Getting to know you activity:** This will help the learners co-create a friendly learning space together.

Here are some FAQs surrounding pre-course surveys:

- **What's the best way to do a pre-course survey?** It really depends on the learners and the 'classroom' situation – you can get them to fill in an online survey, make it a silent written activity in class, or you can send them a document to fill out and return to you as a 'take home' task. It's fairly simple to set up an online survey using software such as Google Forms or SurveyMonkey.
- **Can you do it as a group activity?** A more engaging way might be to do the activity as a group on day 1 so you all get to know each other. You can use a 'brainstorming station' or a 'speed dating'[7] type of activity, moving learners every few minutes so they can get to know more people, more quickly, in a fun, lively environment. Remember – if running a group activity, make sure you let learners know before they start that they can email you with any sensitive information or barriers that they don't want to share in the group.
- **How do you do 'getting to know you' activities when your learners are online?** Another good question! If you have a forum or chat facility, post a little about yourself by answering three questions of

your choosing – and then invite others to do the same. If you're in a live online meeting, you can do the same or put smaller groups into breakout rooms to introduce themselves, before introducing each other to the group. You can also set up questions on an app such as Mentimeter or Kahoot!, where you give everyone a time limit to answer a question, before revealing a summary of the responses to the whole group. Apps like these are brilliant for getting everyone engaged in a very quick and responsive way. Have a series of questions they can answer one after the other, so you can alternate between quiet time (when they're responding) and discussion.

- **What if the first time you meet your learners is the first day of the course and you don't have time to make changes to the course?** The beauty of online learning (and digital workplaces) is that you usually have some lead time, so send reminder emails in the days leading up to the course to remind learners to fill out the questionnaires before commencing where possible. If for some reason you can't do this before the first time you meet them online, or you are meeting them for the first time face to face, you have an awesome opportunity to integrate some questions from the survey into your first session. Instantly, your audience will know that your first priority is to get to know them as people – and the trust and rapport can begin to be built. The more you know about your learners, the better you can adapt.

What does a pre-course questionnaire look like?

On the Resources page, I've included a link to a questionnaire I send to prospective clients – access this if you'd like to see an example. The questionnaire you use really depends on what type of course or workshop you're running, as to how much and what type of information you'd like to know about your learners before you start working with them.

Practical application – your turn!

Creating needs-based training solutions has two parts – understanding your learners, and mixing up activity types to cater for different needs.

Practical task 1a: Create a learner profiling tool

- Create a survey tool or profiling tool you can use with your learners or clients to find out more about their experience, goals, barriers to learning and preferred learning styles. At a minimum, this survey should include questions regarding:
  - their experience in your field
  - their motivations or goals for learning with you
  - any personal circumstances that will make doing homework tasks difficult, or prevent the learner from attending class
  - any cultural, behavioural or medical considerations for classroom-based activities
  - the technology they are familiar with and use on a daily basis
  - the generation they identify with
  - their pronouns
  - how they prefer to learn (such as in groups, alone, listening, watching or reading).
- Consider:
  - What's the best way for you to use your profiling tool? When and how will you send it?
  - If you're teaching a group, how will you get the group to know more about each other?
  - If you're in an organisation, do you have the results of a recent training needs analysis that can inform whether the needs of the learners are aligned with organisational goals? Have you considered the needs of all potential stakeholders?

Practical task 1b: Expand your activity type profile

Once you've found out more about your learners' learning styles, think about the styles that you do and don't cater for in your lessons, and then work on integrating a wider range of activities into your lesson planning. Mix it up! Variety is what keeps a class engaged long-term, so if you're stuck in a lecturing rut, throw in some discussions, problem-solving and critical-thinking activities – your learners will thank you.

If you're stumped as to what kinds of activities you could add to your lessons, go back to the pages provided on multiple intelligences and learning styles in the previous sections – or ask your favourite search engine. Use prompts that describe your learners, such as, 'What activities are good for spatial learners?' or 'What learning activities are better for millennials?'

Key takeaways

Here's a summary of the key points in this chapter:

- Learners have different needs, so it's important that we get to know them and their motivations for learning, previous experience, any barriers that may affect their learning, and the ways they find learning easiest.
- Doing this before you begin teaching helps to create a safe, trusted space in which learners know your priority is shaping the learning experience to their needs, instead of using a cookie-cutter approach and treating them the same as any other learner you've had.
- Mixing up the learning experience to include as many different types of activities as possible means you're appealing to as wide a range of learners as possible.
- If you're in a group learning environment, making sure the learners are getting to know each other is important. The more you all know about each other and the ways you learn best, the more trusted, open and communicative the environment will be in which you're learning.

Chapter 1 reflection

Check your answers to the initial pre-test (stage 1 diagnostic) – how much have you learnt? What are your biggest takeaways from this chapter? What will you do differently?

CHAPTER 2

Set clear expectations of the learning experience

The outcome

Set clear expectations of the learning experience

The why

Why is it important to set clear expectations of the learning experience?

Because, quite simply, not a single learner in the world wants to feel ripped off, over-sold, like they're wasting their time or they haven't got a fair outcome for the amount of time, money and effort they've put into your learning experience – be that a presentation, a course or a whole degree program.

What happens when you don't set clear expectations of the learning experience?

Your learners get annoyed, disengaged or, at worst, lodge formal complaints against you. They might be upset because they:

- thought they were getting more, or having to do less
- didn't realise they had to spend more on equipment or tools than they had budgeted (and that includes things such as access to a solid wifi connection or data allowance if you're expecting them to do homework tasks)
- didn't realise how much time they'd have to spend studying, preparing for assessments or fulfilling the minimum requirements
- thought they'd be getting more one-to-one support
- thought they'd get more feedback or guidance with practical application or assessment tasks.

The list could go on and on.

CHAPTER 2: Set clear expectations of the learning experience ■ 43

Do you want to be the facilitator who is on the receiving end of that kind of feedback?

I assume not. The feeling is much like buying a product that doesn't deliver on what you thought it would, or an experience falling short because the expectations were unrealistic. Whether it's as a consumer or as a learner, no-one wants to feel duped.

Likely you can relate to buying a product that falls short of your expectations, but have you had that experience as a learner as well? If you're struggling to understand what it feels like to be in that position, here's a real life example for you.

I recently finished a master's degree in Norway. During one of the units, we didn't get the assessment criteria until week seven of the 12-week course. Week *seven*. And you might think, *Well, if the assessments are due in week 12, that's not too bad, is it?*

Yes, it is. We had no idea why we were turning up to lectures, what we were supposed to be listening for, remembering or being able to debate about. We were feverishly trying to take down notes on *everything*, constantly wondering whether a particular lecture or reading would end up being 'tested' in the assessment. This created an enormous amount of extra work and stress for all of us. We were second-guessing ourselves continuously; do we even need to know this? In how much detail do we need to understand it? Do we just need a base understanding or to be able to debate the details? Having that criteria right at the start would have saved us so much time and so much confusion.

When we finally did get the assessment criteria, it was so confusing and contradictory it had to be rewritten by the lecturers. This meant we didn't actually find out how we were being assessed until week 9. Week *nine* of a 12-week course. You can imagine the amount of pressure that put us all under – having just a few short weeks to pull our assessments together when this was only *one* of four units we were studying concurrently.

Some people in our course had a lot riding on whether they got top marks (for further PhD opportunities); without A-grade level results, their chosen career path would essentially be stripped away from them. Can you imagine the stress they were under already, without the disorganisation of the department amplifying that tenfold?

This was a core unit in the degree, so we also really started to question whether we should be continuing with the program at all. This was an incredibly debasing experience that eroded our faith in the entire institution. Is that how you want your learners to feel? Stressed, confused and second-guessing whether they should have invested their time with you?

> You cannot set clear expectations for your learners,
> if these expectations are still unclear to *you*.

So what's the solution? You create a solid course (or presentation) outline that answers all those questions up front, to set you and your learners up on a solid, trusted foundation before you even get started.

> Build a strong foundation and you can reach
> even the most unthinkable heights.
>
> MJ Moores

Core concepts 'pre-test' – do you really need this chapter?

If you've already done the stage 1 diagnostic, you can skip over the skills and knowledge checks, and start at the section, 'The "what, when and how" (the theory)'. If you haven't done the online diagnostic, answer the following questions.

SKILLS CHECK: How much are you already doing?

Find the practical task at the end of this chapter and see how many boxes you can tick. Options are provided for presentations and whole courses.

KNOWLEDGE CHECK: Which of the following statements do you think are true? Can you explain the reasons for your choices?

1. It's not necessary to know all the outcomes or expectations of the course before your learners enrol. You can figure that out as you go through the course.

2. It's best to give a comprehensive course outline after learners have enrolled.
3. If you're only giving an hour-long presentation, covering off on the outcomes before you start has no benefit and takes time away from delivering the actual content (and they'll get that information soon enough anyway during the presentation).
4. Presentations don't require practical tasks or outcomes because they're not long enough to warrant them.
5. Telling learners when and how to ask questions before you start your presentation or course is a good idea.
6. Learners need to be clear about how they're going to be assessed before they start the course.

If you're unsure about the categories in the practical task, or are not confident explaining why the knowledge check statements are true or false, this chapter is for you!*

The 'what, when and how' (the theory)

We're going to break this section down into what expectations you need to cover for presentations versus courses or programs. Why? Because they are very different beasts!

What expectations should you cover before starting a presentation?

Presentations are a little simpler than whole courses because they're much shorter in nature. At a bare minimum at the start of a presentation, covering off on some basic elements is a good idea so you can set clear expectations of what's coming up. Here's what to provide information on:

- **Why are the learners there?** What's the specific pain point or issue you're addressing? What's the benefit of learners staying engaged until the end? What issue will you help provide a solution for?

---

* Knowledge check answers: Statements 5 and 6 are correct. The others are not correct. You'll find out why during the chapter!

- **What will they be able to do differently?** What will your audience be able to do with the new information? What's the point of knowing this new information? What practical application does it have in their everyday life?
- **How long will it take?** How many hours is the audience expected to be 'present'? Is a break provided?
- **Where does it fit?** Is this part one of a series of presentations? Is it an introduction or a follow-up to another presentation? Is the skills or knowledge level beginner, intermediate or advanced? Who is it intended for? Where does it fit in the grand scheme of your field of expertise?
- **How and when can learners ask questions?** Is a Q&A included at the end, or are learners invited to ask questions whenever something comes up? The audience needs to know when and how to ask for clarification if required.

What expectations should you cover before starting a course, event or longer series of presentations?

Every course, program or event is different. This list is by no means exhaustive, but intended to help you brainstorm the different types of questions your learner may have about how the learning experience operates.

Cover off on these items in your course outline, terms and conditions, sales page or invitation email. If the course outline is delivered before or directly after enrolment, the learner will have the opportunity to decide whether the course is the correct fit and, if not, be able to withdraw (or decide not to enrol) in a timely manner. Wouldn't you prefer to know this information up-front as a learner *before* you enrol? I know I would.

Here's the kind of information to provide to learners:

1. **Content and outcomes:**
   - What theory will you cover?
     - Are the modules clear with topics and/or outcomes stated?
     - Are 'rest' or 'catch-up' weeks scheduled into the program?
   - What outcomes or competencies are they aiming to achieve for each module?

- Does each module include a practical task that guarantees the outcome?
- Are the tasks your learners will be able to *do* after finishing the course clear?
- How does this learning align with organisational or industry requirements (or their professional development pathway)?
- Are any pre-requisite skills or knowledge necessary for understanding the course content?
  - Should they be familiar with any books, websites or manuals?
  - Should they be following or familiar with any groups, organisations, websites or mailing lists?
  - Are any previous modules or qualifications required?

2. **Equipment and tools required:**
   - What software and hardware do they require?
     - Apps? Google account? Microsoft account?
     - Microphone? Laptop? Headphones?
   - What tools or equipment do they need?
     - Industry-specific requirements should be included here (such as personal protective equipment for tradespeople).
   - What connectivity do they need outside of the 'classroom' to complete their homework/pre-learning/assessment tasks?
     - Wifi, 5G network?
     - Bandwidth and download requirements? (Often learners won't have unlimited internet access like they would if they were at work or college, so it's important for learners to be able to predict whether this will incur further costs or access issues for them.)
   - What support materials are available?
     - These could include handouts, recorded tutorials, online learning platform, workbooks, training manuals and training videos.

3. **Delivery mode and expected involvement:**
   - Where and how will the content be delivered?
     - Face to face – time, date and place?
     - Online – time, date and place, and via which streaming software or platform, or self-study only?

- Blended – a mix of face to face and online, or self-study and live online?
- Is a session-by-session, day-by-day or week-by-week schedule of content available?
- How long should the course take to get through (days, weeks, months)?
- How many hours per day/week/month should the client need to allocate to study, active involvement, forum participation or homework tasks? If the course is mandatory for work, is time allocated in the working day for study or is it expected to be done outside of work hours?
- What involvement is expected?
  - Face-to-face meetings?
  - Online webinars or tutorials?
  - Fixed time and place or 'self-directed' (at learners' own pace)?
  - One-on-one time with a mentor or supervisor?
  - Group work or buddy system with other participants?
- How many other learners are in their 'cohort'? (That is, how many other people do they have to share the time of the facilitator with? Or participate in groups with?) For sensitive topics or subjects, learners may prefer smaller group settings or want the level of support only small groups can provide.
- How long are the materials available for?
  - Does access 'expire' after a certain period of time?
  - Can they join future cohorts for a 'refresher'?
  - What kind of 'homework' or pre-learning do they need to complete before coming to 'classes'?

4. **Communication and support:**
   - Is the content one-way or two-way?
     - One-way: Self-study mode or learner accesses as needed.
     - Two-way: Some involvement with other participants or facilitator.
   - Is there a set time or way to seek feedback or ask questions?
     - During sessions? At the end of sessions?
     - Via email, phone or text?

- Is there a limit to the email, phone or face-to-face support you give as the facilitator?
    - Consider the frequency, volume and expected amount of support to be provided.
- How should learners approach you if they have issues that prevent them from fully participating or making use of the materials?
- If they have to submit tasks or assessments, where and how do they do that?
- If they have discussions or live webinars to participate in, how, where and when do they do that?

5. **Assessment and feedback:**
    - What tasks should they be completing?
        - Is a certain length or complexity expected for each task?
        - What are the marking or assessment criteria? Does the learner know how to 'pass' the assessment or achieve high grades?
        - When are assessments due?
        - What happens if they're overdue?
    - Do they get feedback on their tasks?
    - How do they get that feedback? (Personally, in a group, written or oral?)
    - When can they expect feedback?

One more quick story to reinforce how incredibly important it is to provide clear assessment criteria. Remember that master's degree I did in Norway? In one unit we were told that we could write a paper on any topic we liked, as long as it was aligned with one of the 12 topics that the lecturer delivered over the 12-week term. The unit had no other assessment. Aside from being an ingenious way to encourage students to attend only one out of 12 lectures, it also put a lot of pressure on us as learners to produce one piece of work that would dictate our grade for the entire unit. (Remember those students who needed top marks because they were pursuing PhDs? Yeah, no pressure.) I was the brave student who asked the lecturer what the assessment criteria would be so that we could understand how to achieve a high grade. His answer was simply, 'Answer a question that is on topic'. Hmmm.

Having been an academic writing skills teacher at university level in Australia, I had marked literally thousands of essays, and always with a very comprehensive set of criteria against which to grade, including but not limited to essay conventions (introduction, body, conclusion), argument structure, paragraph structure, grammar, referencing conventions, coherence and clarity. Some learners would score highly in some areas and lower in others; the whole point of thorough assessment and grading criteria being that learners could isolate what they needed to work on and improve those areas – or not. It's up to the learner really, but at least they have a framework so they know *how* to pass or how to excel if that's their aim.

Without such a structure, I worked on this essay harder than any essay I'd ever written. I gave myself a crash course in Australian refugee politics and spent eight weeks honing my knowledge and finding more evidence to support my arguments. I'm a writer through and through, always have been, and absolutely love the challenge of sculpting, honing and refining a piece of writing until it says exactly what I want it to communicate. I also *love* getting feedback and improving where I can, being a dedicated lifelong learner.

Imagine my disappointment when I received the paper back with a C grade and no feedback. Now I wasn't expecting an A grade, but C equated to 'satisfactory' and considering the amount of effort I'd put into this piece of work, I wanted to know where I could have improved. Was it the quality of the argument? The depth of the referencing? Coherence or clarity? I knew how to ace an essay, so I was confused.

I asked the lecturer for feedback, to which he replied that his decision was final and discussion would not be entered into. Being a specialist in education and training, and infuriated by the process and the lack of transparency around how the grade was achieved, I lodged a formal complaint with the university board. The paper was graded again by an external examiner, and this time returned with a D grade – one level above a fail grade, and again without any justification or criteria against which it was graded. The only comment was, 'It appears this paper was thrown together overnight', which was most definitely not the case. This just led me to feel punished for asking for feedback and, again, questioning whether I should be bothering with the rest of the degree.

CHAPTER 2: Set clear expectations of the learning experience ■ 51

I was absolutely livid with the entire process but determined to prove how ridiculous the policies of the university were, so for the next unit I resubmitted virtually the same paper (paraphrasing all the paragraphs so I couldn't be caught for self-plagiarism, but using identical references and arguments). The paper was given an A grade by the head of the department, with comments saying how thoroughly thought through and compelling the arguments were. Go figure. #facepalm

Was the paper worth an A grade or a D grade? Three different academics, three different opinions. If I had been going for a PhD, this anomaly would have completely derailed my career. Luckily, I had no desire to pursue a PhD or become an academic. (And if you ever hear me even *hint* at the possibility of this happening, please send help immediately!) My point is to highlight how incredibly destructive not having clear assessment criteria can be. Are you setting your learners up for failure or success? Assessment shouldn't be a guessing game for the learner or the assessor. Full stop.

Demonstrate with clear examples

> So do I have some examples to show you? Well, no. Not course outline or sales page examples anyway. I think the easiest way for you to see this in action is to go and find yourself some examples in the wild! Next time you're signing up for a course, a webinar or a presentation (or looking at what information you provide to your own learners), check how much information is actually provided prior to signing up.

Does this information change whether you'd invest or sign up? Do the unanswered questions leave you considering whether value exists in the time and cost investment? Are you questioning the integrity or organisation of the person behind the course? Are you wondering whether the lack (or depth) of information provided is an indication of how well prepared they are to teach?

> **A lack of transparency results in distrust
> and a deep sense of insecurity.**
>
> Dalai Lama

The Dalai Lama is right – do you want to create that safe, secure, trusted space with your learners from the very outset, or do you want to do what that Norwegian lecturer did to me?

Being transparent about the expectations around your course or program simply helps prospective learners ensure that they're choosing the right course, and sets you and your learners up on a solid foundation.

Practical application – your turn!

Assess your own presentations and courses for how well you set expectations. How clear is your documentation about what to expect from you and your presentations or courses?

Practical task 2a: Checklist for presentation outlines

Ensure you've covered the following:
- why your learners are there (what they're going to achieve)
- what practical tasks they will be able to do differently by the end of your presentation
- how long it's expected to take
- how and when to ask questions.

Practical task 2b: Checklist for course outlines

The bulk of this chapter focused on five core areas that should be covered in your course outlines. I have created a questionnaire for you (available on the Resources page) that can help you brainstorm out your own course outline, sales page or terms and conditions document. How much of your course outlines can be improved or added to?

CHAPTER 2: Set clear expectations of the learning experience

Key takeaways

Transparency builds trust with learners and prevents dissatisfaction; using the practical checklists provided in this chapter allows you to ensure you're giving learners all the information they need.

Remember:
- Clear expectations create trust and ultimately higher satisfaction ratings.
- Unclear expectations lead to frustration and disengagement.
- Presentations require basic expectation-setting, while courses and longer programs require more comprehensive expectations.
- You cannot set clear expectations if outcomes are unclear to you – know your content and structure thoroughly before promising outcomes to learners.

Chapter 2 reflection

Check your answers to the initial pre-test (stage 1 diagnostic) – how much have you learnt? What are your biggest takeaways from this chapter? What will you do differently?

CHAPTER 3

Implement the 'test-teach-test' paradigm

The outcome

Implement the 'test-teach-test' paradigm

The why

Why is discovery-based structure the key to engagement?

Discovery-based structure is all about getting your learners involved, instead of just being passive observers in the learning process. You want learners to be motivated to fill the gaps in their skills and knowledge. You want them engaged, focused, looking for answers and eager to use their new knowledge and skills.

They don't want to be firehosed with information they already know, or bombarded with more facts and figures than they can process in a single afternoon. You don't want them falling asleep, half engaged, giving themselves manicures or writing their shopping list out of sheer boredom (like I remember doing through countless lectures before we had devices and the internet to keep us occupied).

> **Putting learners in the driver's seat (through discovery-based learning) is the key to them retaining knowledge and being motivated to apply it in the real world.**

Have you ever heard of information gap theory? Coined by neuro-economist George Loewenstein in 1994 (neuroeconomics combines insights from neuroscience, psychology and economics), the theory can be applied to anything from economics to marketing. However, the core premise of this theory is that identifying a gap in information creates curiosity, which then creates a desire to take action to fill that gap.

Allowing learners to discover gaps in their knowledge and then drive their own learning process allows them to question, think and discover – instead of being on autopilot in the learning process. Using the test-teach-test paradigm when you're creating learning experiences allows you to identify such gaps.

What is the test-teach-test paradigm?

Consider these two scenarios as a learner. Which scenario would you prefer to be part of?

1. **Teach-test:** Turn up for a lecture and sit through 90 minutes of information. Realise at the end that you actually already knew most of it. Many people would be pretty miffed if that was the case. We all lead busy lives and few people enjoy having their time wasted. It might also seriously dissuade them from turning up to another of this person's lectures.
2. **Test-teach-test:** Turn up for a lecture, and the lecturer starts off with 15 questions, telling you, 'If you think you can answer them fully and are confident with this topic, you might be better off skipping this one. You might pick up a few bits and pieces here and there but please don't feel obliged to stay if you don't think you're going to get a lot from this class'.

In this scenario, people are going to do one of two things:
1. realise they can't answer the questions and be motivated to stay
2. realise they can answer (most of) the questions and decide it's not a good use of their time.

People in the second group will then do one of two things:
1. leave or hang out at the back half-listening
2. stick around to fill in the gaps in their knowledge.

What happens when you don't use the test-teach-test paradigm?

You run the very real risk of teaching a chef how to fry eggs. (Wo)mansplaining what they already know. Preaching to the choir. Singing from the same song sheet. #EnoughWithTheCliches. Whose face is the egg on in that scenario? The teacher. Not the learner.

In my experience I've found that when given the opportunity to leave, 95 per cent of the time, people will stay. It's human nature to want to stick around and confirm what you know, and *bonus* if you pick up something new, right?

So give people the option to leave

Or invite them to sit at the back of the class doing other work if they'd like to have half an ear open but not be fully involved in the class.

Some might leave, but most will have more respect for you as a facilitator, and they'll be much more likely to turn up to your next presentation.

Before we go on, ask yourself the following simple question.

Do you want to be a 'lecturer' or a 'facilitator of learning'?

What is the difference? These aren't textbook definitions, but more an indication of what I mean when I use them in this book:

- A **lecturer** provides a lot of information, monologue style, and has little interaction with the audience.
- A **facilitator** also might provide a lot of information, but they interact heavily with the audience, asking questions, posing problems to solve, providing practical ways to apply knowledge right there and then in the class. They provide a pathway through the information so learners can *use* that new knowledge in the real world.

> What do you want to be? A lecturer? Or a facilitator of learning? If you aspire to be a facilitator of learning, test-teach-test is the core paradigm around which you want to base your entire teaching practice.

Core concepts 'pre-test' – do you really need this chapter?

I wouldn't be practising what I'm preaching if I didn't have a pre-test for you, now would I? If you've already done the stage 1 diagnostic, you can skip over the skills and knowledge checks, and start at the section, 'The "what, when and how" (the theory)'. If you haven't done the online diagnostic, answer the following questions.

SKILLS CHECK: How much are you already doing?
- Asking learners to participate in reflective activities prior to learning.
- Using questions in the titles of all presentation slides.
- Asking learners to brainstorm before providing answers.
- Making the learning a quiz – so they're discovering answers, not being told the answers.
- Asking learners to look out for the answers to questions before reading a text or watching a video.
- Removing strategic parts of the learning content – so learners have to figure out what the missing pieces are.
- Using a combination of reflection, comprehension and application-based activities in workbooks.
- Using apps to ascertain prior knowledge.

KNOWLEDGE CHECK: Which of the following statements do you think are true? Can you explain the reasons for your choices?
1. You only implement the test-teach-test strategy at the start and end of a lesson.
2. Starting with a reflective activity is an example of a test-teach-test strategy.
3. Titles of slides or sections should be questions as often as possible, if not all the time.
4. You don't have to present learning content – providing a test instead is just as effective, if not more effective.
5. You should always provide questions *before* asking learners to read or watch something.
6. Workbooks are not a way of implementing the test-teach-test strategy.

If you're unsure about using the listed skills, or are not confident explaining why the knowledge check statements are true or false, this chapter is for you!*

The 'what, when and how' (the theory)

What exactly is the 'test-teach-test' paradigm?

Essentially, the 'test-teach-test' paradigm is about not teaching anything until you know the learners have a gap in their knowledge. The process is as follows:

- **Test** to find out how much they already know.
- **Teach** them what they don't know.
- **Test** them again to find out how much they've learnt.

It's that simple. This way, you avoid having to teach things they already know, saving you and them time and energy. Who doesn't want that?

So we just give them a test at the start and end of the class?

No. It's much more than that.

It's all about asking questions – lots of questions.

The aim is to see what prior knowledge they have at every stage of the lesson, before spoonfeeding your learners the answers. That way, their 'discovery-learning brain' is turned on and they're eager to find out whether they're right or wrong – it's simple human nature.

So how about we practise what we preach?

Think back through the chapters you've read so far in this book. Think about all of the times you were 'tested' before the learning content was presented to you. Think about all the questions I've asked.

How many ways have you seen the test-teach-test paradigm being implemented? If you're not sure, flick through the parts you've already read – are you seeing a pattern?

(See, I'm doing it now – getting you to think about it for yourself before I reveal the answers …)

---

* Knowledge check answers: Statements 1 and 6 are incorrect. The others are correct. You'll find out why during the chapter!

Demonstrate with clear examples

How do we implement the test-teach-test paradigm in every lesson?

I've got five clear ways you can implement the test-teach-test paradigm in every lesson or presentation you facilitate. After you've read each example, consider whether you could use it with your learners.

Can you start with a reflective activity?

A reflective activity before a lesson starts (using questions to help learners consider what they already know – in the case of this book, the diagnostics), will activate prior knowledge.

Why would you want to do that? This is an example of constructivism in action – the theory of learning that (among other things) proposes that you learn something new only by 'attaching' it to something else you already know. Although the three foundational psychologists of constructivism – Jean Piaget, Lev Vygotsky and John Dewey – all studied different aspects of this theory, one of the core tenets held by all three was the concept that activating prior knowledge was the key to making meaning out of theory, and retaining new knowledge.

The added bonus to starting a class with a reflective activity is that, as the teacher, you find out which learners have experience and knowledge in certain areas – and you can draw on this later to help you in the classroom (more on that technique later).

Telling chefs how to fry eggs? Unnecessary! Can you start your presentation with a quick reflective activity to get people's prior knowledge activated?

Can you make your slide titles questions as often as possible?

When you do this, the question you're answering is always there in front of the learners. This means even if they drift off or get distracted, they're always aware of what answers they should be looking out for. Even in this section, I've used questions for the headings – instead of, say, highlighting a 'strategy' such as 'Make your slide titles questions as often as possible'. Have a look at all five strategies in this section and flick through the previous pages in the book. How many questions can you see? That's right – they're everywhere, and for good reason.

If you're asked a question, you naturally already have an answer popping up in your head that you want verification of. Again, wanting to know whether you're right or wrong is a simple case of human nature – and that's why you'll stay and listen to or read through the rest of that section!

Say, for example, I asked you, 'How old do you think I am?'

You're probably either thinking, *Oh dear, is this a trick question?* (haha) or, more than likely, based on how much you know about me, a number is popping up into your head. The answer will either be close to what you thought or way off – and *that* is what you'll remember. You'll remember the number, because it was either so different or so similar to what you already thought.

How many of your slide titles could be questions? (*Hint:* Rarely can a slide not begin with a question.) Remember information gap theory – if learners know they have a gap in knowledge, they'll be eager to find out what the answer is!

Can you create activities that make learners brainstorm possible answers *before* providing the learning content?

Again, this helps the learner access their prior knowledge, make educated guesses and prepare themselves for finding out how close they were to the right answers. This is a far more effective teaching technique than simply shovelling information at students with no interactivity or engagement. This way they're actively thinking, not just passively absorbing, and that makes for a much more memorable learning experience. For example, you could use the following process:

- Put some key questions into an online anonymous survey app (or write them on the board).
- Ask learners to respond in real time, so they can see all the possible answers pop up from their classmates in the app or on the board (or answers could be passed up to the front and added to the board anonymously).
- You could then try any of the following:
  - ask the learners to debate which answers they think are correct
  - assign each answer to a different learner and give them five minutes to search online and see if they can prove or disprove the answer to be correct
  - split the class into groups of three and ask each group to decide on the top three correct answers.

All of these suggestions have the same thing in common: you're asking the learner to find the answers, instead of keeping the onus on you as the teacher to provide the answers. Can you do this in your presentations or classes?

Can you create a discovery-based learning activity out of your lecture content?

In this scenario, you're providing the learning material for learners but chopping it up into pieces so they have to figure out how it goes together; this way, they're teaching themselves the content and you don't actually have to do the teaching at all. Try providing the learning material inside a knowledge check activity instead of actually presenting it – that way they're teaching themselves the content and you don't actually have to do the teaching at all. #win–win

You can use discovery-based learning by creating:

- **Mix and match activities:** Provide definitions on one side of a page, and the terminology on the other. Learners test their knowledge by matching the pairs.

- **'True or false' statements:** If written carefully, 'true or false' activities can really test a learner's ability to apply new knowledge to different situations and scenarios.
- **Multiple response quizzes:** These are much more challenging than multiple choice activities because more than one correct answer might be possible – for example, the activity might be to 'tick all the statements that are "true"' (as with the knowledge check questions in this book). Learners need far better depth of understanding to decide which statements are true, rather than isolating the only true statement.
- **Fill the gap activities:** These activities are where you can replace key words or concepts with blank spaces, so the learners have to figure out what the missing pieces are.
- **Scenario-based activities:** This is where you put theory to the test. Put learners in a situation where they have to apply their new knowledge – for example, if you've been teaching first aid, the scenario could involve finding an injured person, giving the learner four options and asking what they should do first. If they get the right answer, they move on. If they don't, they find out why it wasn't right, and then go back and try another scenario until they get the right answer. The more they get 'wrong', the more they'll understand the reasons behind the right answers.

Can you use parts of your learning content as a discovery-based learning activity – instead of lecturing about it?

Can you provide questions before offering a reading, listening or watching activity – so learners know *why* they're engaging with the task?
I'll practise what I preach here, and demonstrate instead of explaining this point. You're going to be presented with a 'process', and you have to remember the key information. Don't take notes, just read as usual.

Involve the learner in 'safe space' practice

In this section, I present the process in two different ways. The first way of learning is akin to most traditional teaching methods – teaching first, and then testing later. The second way of learning demonstrates the test-teach-test strategy. Play along with me – the penny will drop after this activity if it hasn't already!

Way of learning 1: Traditional teach-test

Today, we're going to learn about how to prolong the life of a sewing machine.

A sewing machine is an investment. Whether you use it every day or every once in a while, taking good care of your machine is important.

Performing routine maintenance tasks and keeping your sewing machine clean can add years to its life, so here are our top five tips:

1. **Keep your sewing machine covered.** Dust is the enemy of machinery. To keep your machine as clean as possible, store it under a dust cover or in a hard case.
2. **Change needles regularly.** It's easy to forget how much work your needle does over time. The needle can become dull, which can lead to looped threads, skipped stitches and pulls in the fabric, and potentially damage the machine. Experts recommend changing your needle every eight hours or every time you complete a project. You also might need to change the needle to match the weight and weave of the fabric you're using.
3. **Use compressed air to remove lint.** Compressed air can help remove lint and thread from feed dogs, tension discs and the bobbin area. When using compressed air, make sure the nozzle is at least 10 centimetres away from the machine. Keeping the nozzle a fair distance away will help ensure you don't introduce moisture into the machine.
4. **Schedule in regular servicing.** To keep your machine in tiptop shape, make a point of having it professionally serviced each year. A knowledgeable and experienced service person will adjust the timing and tension, and clean the areas of your machine that you can't get to without taking the entire machine apart. Your machine's

life will be greatly extended if you have it serviced by a professional from time to time.
5. **Oil the machine.** Like most other machines, sewing machines benefit from regular oiling. Sewing machines have a lot of internal moving parts. Oiling the machine will help these parts run smoother and for longer. Sewing machine oil can be purchased online or from most craft stores, and is designed specifically for use with sewing machines. Never use anything but sewing machine oil in your machine.

Now, answer these questions about how to prolong the life of your sewing machine, without reading back over the tips provided.
1. Why should you regularly service your machine?
2. Why should you keep your machine covered?
3. Why and how should you change your needle?
4. What's the best way of removing lint from your machine?
5. Should you get your machine serviced and if so how often?
6. Which type of oil should you use for your machine?

Unless you're a sewing machine enthusiast, how hard is it to recall all of that information without going back over the core content?

Way of learning 2: Test-teach-test

Now imagine the same activity, but I provided you with those core concepts questions *before* you read the text. Wouldn't that have been easier?

This is the reality of what happens when you deliver a whole bunch of information to your learner, and then expect them to recall important points. Providing the questions before learners read, watch or listen gives them a focus when engaging with the material – and so they have a much higher chance of finding the important information and retaining that knowledge.

Give it a go yourself. Now that you've got the questions, how quickly can you find the answers? It's way easier, isn't it?

Now ask yourself:
1. Which way of learning do you think makes it easier to retain more knowledge? Way 1 (teach-test) or way 2 (test-teach-test)?
2. Which way do you think is more fun and interactive for learners?
3. Which way do you think is more fun to deliver?

The answer to all three questions, as far as I'm concerned, is way 2: test-teach-test. It's all about making your learners *think*.

Carve up your content in a way that will help them discover answers, not just passively absorb them. If you're asking questions *before* they get the new knowledge, consider getting them to brainstorm their answers with their peers. Finding out whether you're right or wrong when you're predicting answers is always more fun than just passively trying to absorb new information.

Can apps help too?

Yes! A myriad of apps can help you if you're running face to face or online workshops. You don't need to present the learning content if your learners can provide or predict it for themselves, right?

Using the third strategy just outlined (creating activities or surveys that you can drop into your training *before* delivering content) will give your learners a chance to *think* before you feed them the content, and you a chance to find out what they already know. You can also use such quizzes to test their knowledge *after* you've delivered the learning content, to see how much they've learnt.

Google Forms, Mentimeter and Kahoot! are just a few options here. I'm not going to spend time teaching you how to use them because, firstly, their websites do that and, secondly, you can use so many apps for this purpose, so it's really up to you to find the ones you like the best!

Are workbooks another way of implementing the test-teach-test paradigm?

Yes! Workbooks provide an excellent opportunity to put the test-teach-test paradigm into practice. Use workbooks to provide a place for learners to brainstorm their existing knowledge and record new knowledge. I don't have a workbook as part of this book, but I have posed a lot of questions, reflections and activities for you to do in your own time, haven't I?

Look back through the book now. Can you find examples of the following activity types?

Here are the three types of activities that are common in workbooks:
- **Reflection activities:** To brainstorm prior knowledge or future application.
- **Comprehension activities:** To record new knowledge and learning content.
- **Application activities:** To apply new knowledge in real-life scenarios.

If a workbook was included with this book these are the questions it would have:
1. Why is it important to test knowledge *before* you teach it, and then test it again afterwards? Why is discovery-based structure the key to engagement? To what extent and *how* are you already doing this in your online learning materials?
2. What is the test-teach-test paradigm?
3. What are five ways you can implement test-teach-test into your presentations or lessons?
4. Describe the ways that you can adapt your existing learning materials to include the five strategies.
5. How can you use online apps to help you implement a test-teach-test approach?
6. How does a workbook help you to implement the test-teach-test paradigm?
7. What are the three types of activities you can put into a workbook?

The first two questions are reflection questions, and the rest of the questions are comprehension questions – the application questions are included in the next section.

Notice that the questions are literally a summary of this chapter, and that they're also the skills check questions in the diagnostic.

If this chapter were a presentation, those questions would also be the titles of my slides.

Are you seeing a pattern here? Questions really are the key to driving a discovery-based learning experience.

Questions are everything.

Practical application – your turn!

Ready to put all this into action?

Practical task 3a: Integrate standard test-teach-test activities

Incorporating the following types of activities into your presentations and courses will ensure you are using the test-teach-test strategy:
- **Test:** Use reflection or pre-course quiz activities to brainstorm prior knowledge or future application.
- **Teach:** Include comprehension activities to record new knowledge and learning content.
- **Test:** Add in application or post-course activities to apply new knowledge in real-life scenarios.

Do you have all three types of activities in your courses? If not, can you add them?

Practical task 3b: Use test-teach-test strategies

In this chapter I've presented at least five strategies for implementing the test-teach-test model into your presentations and courses. How many of them do you think you can use?
1. How often can you start with a reflective activity?
2. Can you make your titles and headings questions as often as possible?
3. Where can you create activities that make the learner brainstorm possible answers *before* you provide the learning content?
4. Can you repurpose strategic parts of the learning content as discovery-based learning activities – instead of lecturing about it? Consider the following activities:
    - mix and match activities
    - 'true or false' statements

- multiple response quizzes
- fill the gap activities
- scenario-based activities.
5. Can you provide questions before offering a reading, listening or watching activity – so learners know *why* they're engaging with the task?

Key takeaways

The key takeaways about implementing the test-teach-test paradigm are as follows:
- The test-teach-test paradigm involves:
    - testing learners' knowledge before teaching
    - teaching only what they don't know
    - testing again to confirm learning.
- Using this strategy keeps learners engaged by:
    - putting them in the driver's seat (discovery-based learning)
    - activating prior knowledge (constructivist approach)
    - making learning more interactive and less passive.
- The benefits of using these strategies include:
    - avoiding teaching what learners already know
    - increasing engagement and retention
    - making learning more efficient and respectful of learners' time
    - transforming from 'lecturer' to 'facilitator of learning'.
- The test-teach-test strategy can be implemented in a variety of ways, including using reflective activities, asking questions and getting learners to brainstorm answers before being guided to the answers.

Questions are the key to driving discovery-based learning experiences. They should be integrated throughout the teaching process, and not just at the beginning and end.

> **Chapter 3 reflection**
> Check your answers to the initial pre-test (stage 1 diagnostic) – how much have you learnt? What are your biggest takeaways from this chapter? What will you do differently?

Where to now?

By now, we've got the foundations right: we know who our learners are and how to cater for their needs, they're clear on what the expectations are for the course, their facilitator and themselves, and you're committed to being the kind of facilitator who would prefer not to 'mansplain' how to fry an egg to a chef. Fabulous! Next, we're going to talk about how to structure your lessons or presentations – the process often referred to as 'curriculum development'.

OUTCOME: Ensure consistency, structure and an outcomes-based curriculum

STAGE 2

CONSTRUCT: Curriculum development

Transferring knowledge effectively isn't just about firehosing your learners with theory. Lessons that are well-structured have a much higher chance of 'landing' with your learners, enabling them to use their new knowledge and skills with confidence in the real world. Consciously constructing a curriculum is about weaving a pathway so a learner is hooked from the start and driven to follow the learning journey right through to completion, rather than just being a passive 'passenger' in the process.

Taking this concept of a journey one step further, developing a curriculum overview of a series of lessons is like having a detailed roadmap – without it, you get very lost, very quickly!

When you fail to structure lessons well, or cannot see the core elements of a series of lessons lined up against one another, you run the risk of not being able to deliver on your obligations (be they professional, organisational or industry-mandated). This may be due to gaps in the theory, repetition of concepts or examples, or an imbalance of demonstrations, practical activities or opportunities for competency-based evidence to be collected. None of these things build rapport with your learners, or confidence in you or your organisation as being organised, thorough or well-prepared.

How well-structured is your curriculum?

If you really want to *construct* a solid curriculum, you'll need to:
- create outcomes-based modules of training
- structure your lesson for success
- systemise, consolidate and leverage your expertise.

These coincidentally are covered in the next three chapters. If you're pretty sure you've got this stage covered already, confirm it by doing the stage 2 diagnostic on the Resources page on my website. (Scan the QR code to access.)

If you do 'score' highly, I'd still recommend skimming through the chapters, if only to confirm you're on the right track.

CHAPTER 4
Create outcomes-based modules of learning

The outcome

Create outcomes-based modules of learning

The why

Why is creating outcomes-based modules of learning important?

When learners don't have a goal to work towards, motivation disappears, engagement drops off, and they end up frustrated and bored. This is a great way to get negative feedback, unsavoury reviews, and word of mouth that you're not the right person to work with. I'm assuming if you're reading this book, you'd prefer the opposite to that scenario.

What happens when you do focus on outcomes rather than theory?

Change happens. Learners are able to apply their new knowledge in real-world situations, in real time. Information means nothing without practical application, and with *outcomes*, learners can literally be aiming for and kicking goals in partnership with you.

Focusing on outcomes is the difference between approaching a bunch of teenagers and saying:

- 'Today we're going to learn about tyre punctures.'
  and
- 'Today you're going to learn how to repair three types of tyre punctures – when you can either write down or tell me the process for all three, you can go home!'

How much more concrete is the second introduction to the day's learning?

The first class could go on for *hours* – no real definition has been provided of how much you're going to learn about punctures and, to be fair, a lecturer could wax lyrical about that subject for hours on end, boring their learners to tears. In the second option, a clear task to achieve has been outlined, after which you know you can leave. I know which class I'd prefer to be in!

I learnt this lesson the hard way when I was in my early 20s. I joined a gym and got a free personal training session, in which a lovely instructor walked me through a program I could follow three times a week. At no point did she ask me what I wanted to achieve by coming to the gym. If she had asked, I would have told her that my goal (what I wanted to achieve), was to lose weight and tone up.

Unfortunately she didn't ask, and the program I followed led me to actually put *on* a lot of weight due to the amount of muscle I was building. In hindsight, she was super muscly herself, so chances are she thought everyone coming to a gym wanted to put on muscle. The problem was that I didn't. In fact, I was looking for the opposite – to slim down my 5 foot 9 frame, not bulk it up. All I saw after six months of relentlessly following the program was ten kilograms of weight gain – so I promptly cancelled my membership and didn't go back to a gym for the next 20 years. True story. I now love the gym. That's a whole other story. What's the moral of this story, though?

Give your learners a concrete goal to reach and they'll be more motivated to show up and put their money where their mouth is – repair three types of tyre punctures you say? If it means we can get out of here earlier on a Friday afternoon, bring it *on*! Those teens will be paying attention more than you thought possible!

So to what extent are you already doing this when you're in the teaching seat?

Do you list all the:

- **things** they're going to learn about?
- **topics** you're going to cover?
- **outcomes** or **goals** they're going to be working towards?

If you deliver training with learning materials such as slides, videos, audios, online lessons, workbooks or facilitator notes, now's the time to have at least one set either close to hand or front of mind so you can check your own materials against the recommendations that are coming up in this chapter.

Pre-test – do you really need this chapter?

The skills check and knowledge check for this chapter are in the stage 2 diagnostic on the Resources page on my website.

The 'what, when and how' (the theory)

What is an 'outcome' and how do you write a good one?

An outcome is four things:
1. what you can *do* with your new knowledge
2. usually the basis of an assessment or task that proves you are competent in that 'action'
3. verb-based
4. at a specific 'level of thinking'.

Level of what? Thinking.

What are 'levels of thinking' and what do they have to do with the outcomes in your course?

Verbs (doing words) related to thinking and learning can be categorised into various 'levels'. In 1956, educational psychologist Benjamin Bloom headed up a team of educators and researchers to define these levels and develop what's become known as Bloom's taxonomy – shown in the following figure. This model is still used today.

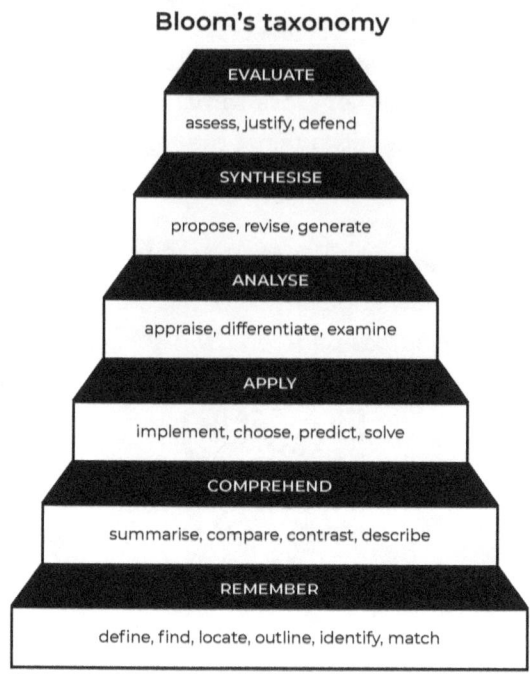

As captured in the model, 'thinking' happens at different levels of complexity. At the lower order, it's all about remembering (or being able to regurgitate) information.

If you think back to your high school tests, you likely remember very little of the information you supposedly 'learnt'. Can you recite all the elements on the periodic table? Label all the bones, organs and cell structures in the body? Name all the geographical terms for the types of rock or list out the events that lead to the end of World War I and II?

I know I can't.

If you can, chances are it's because you're still *using* that knowledge or it's still relevant in your day-to-day work or life. I don't know about you, but I learnt a *lot* of facts at school that I've never had the need nor desire to use since; therefore, because I remembered those facts simply to regurgitate them in an exam, I've since forgotten most of them – is it the same for you?

Depending on the source, the figures do change but the overall reality is clear: cramming for exams does not promote long-term memorisation. Some studies indicate that you can lose up to 70 per cent of what you've learnt within a day, and up to 90 per cent after a week, unless you're reinforcing it regularly or practically applying it. Is that what you want for your learners?

When does real learning happen?

Real learning happens after the 'regurgitation' stage of Bloom's taxonomy, and when you start to do the following:

- **Demonstrate an understanding (*comprehension*):** This includes being able to define, discuss, describe, give examples, or even better still ...
- **Use that new knowledge in a practical situation (*application*):** This means being able to interpret, predict and produce something with that new knowledge.

Can outcomes start with 'understand'?

Now about the verb *understand*. Yes, it's a verb, but it's a challenging word to use when writing outcomes. While it's an easy outcome for the writer, it's not so easy to achieve for the reader. Why? Because it could theoretically appear at any of the levels in Bloom's taxonomy – for example:

- You can understand something well enough to *define* it, right?
- You also have to understand something well enough to *describe* or *discuss* it, yes?
- You also need to understand something to *apply* the knowledge in a practical situation, right? *Predict, produce, use, write*? You need to *understand* the concept to be able to do any of those things, yes?

Here's my golden tip:

> **Do not use the verb *understand* when writing outcome statements.**

Confused yet? I get it. It can be confusing. It can be easier to see this in action – so how about a demonstration? That's coming up next, but just in case you're already an outcome writing ninja, here's a challenge for you.

Humour me for a moment, and imagine you're teaching what healthy food is and isn't to a bunch of teens, mums in their 40s, or seniors – whoever you're more likely to teach on a day-to-day basis.

If you're thinking, *What's food got to do with the teaching and learning I'm doing?*, sometimes it's best to use a simple example first before trying to apply it to more complex topics such as your own.

> Using Bloom's taxonomy, write six outcomes at the six different levels of the model, with six activities that will guarantee those outcomes, for 'understand what healthy food is'. If you can already do this task with confidence, you can skim over the following demonstration and join us after the series of lightbulbs that are coming up.

Demonstrate with clear examples

The statement, **'Understand what healthy food is'** could be interpreted at any of the six levels of Bloom's taxonomy using the following outcomes.

Level 1: REMEMBER	RECOGNISE healthy food.	ACTIVITY: Show me food that is healthy. The learner can point to 'healthy food'.

> Before you go on, think about what the activity might be for the next level – *describe* healthy food.

CHAPTER 4: Create outcomes-based modules of learning ■ 79

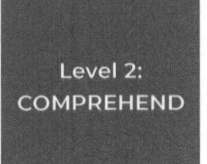

| Level 2: COMPREHEND | DESCRIBE what healthy food is. | ACTIVITY: Tell me *why* that food is healthy. The learner can respond with an explanation like, 'That's healthy food because it's low in fat and sugar, and high in protein'. |

That's the explanation or description level, and a higher order than remember, because the learner can demonstrate *why* the food is healthy, not just point at food that is healthy.

 Before you go on, think about what the activity might be for the next level – *apply* healthy food choices.

| Level 3: APPLY | CHOOSE healthy food options in your weekly meal plan. | ACTIVITY: How can you make sure you choose healthy food options on a regular basis? The learner can respond with a choice like, 'In my normal weekly diet, I'm going to replace fries with boiled potatoes, fried fish with grilled fish, and snack foods with fresh vegetables'. |

Again, this outcome and activity are at a higher level because the learner can now demonstrate how they are going to *use* that new knowledge in their own lives.

 Before you go on, think about what the activity might be for the next level – *analyse* healthy food.

Level 4: ANALYSE	ANALYSE meal plans and decide which ones are healthiest.	ACTIVITY: Out of these four meal plans, which one is healthiest and why? The learner can select the healthiest meal plan and give justifications for why it's healthier than the other three options.

Again, this activity is at a higher level because the learner is demonstrating the ability to analyse a range of plans, rather than just individual foods, and rank items accordingly based on a range of factors.

Before you go on, think about what the activity might be for the next level – *synthesise* healthy food.

Level 5: SYNTHESISE	CREATE a healthy meal plan for a person who has these specific dietary requirements.	ACTIVITY: As it reads in the outcome!

Again, this activity requires a higher level of thinking because the learner is analysing a range of foods for a specific set of circumstances and synthesising them into a bigger project.

Before you go on, think about what the activity might be for the next level – *evaluate* healthy food.

CHAPTER 4: Create outcomes-based modules of learning ■ 81

| Level 6: EVALUATE | EVALUATE a meal plan. | ACTIVITY: Take this meal plan and demonstrate how you would make it healthier, explaining the reasons for your choices in terms of calories, macro balance and nutritional benefit. |

This activity again requires a higher level of thinking because the learner is demonstrating the ability to take a complex set of conditions and assess whether in combination there is room for improvement.

Still think using 'understand' is a good verb for outcomes?

As you can see, 'understand' could be interpreted at a number of different levels of complexity.

How many times have you used 'understand' in your outcomes? How many of them could change?

Need more examples of outcomes?

Think back through the chapters you've read so far, and think of all the times I've presented the outcomes you'll be achieving in this book. Check out the table of contents at the start of this book, for example. What can you see?

You'll see that **every chapter name is actually an outcome statement**.

Have a look at the end of each chapter, before the key takeaways and final reflection sections. What do you see? Practical tasks – which guarantee the outcome promised in that chapter.

Are you ready to have a go at this for your own presentation or course?

That's coming up next, but before that I'd like a quick word on the Australian Qualifications Framework (AQF) – a quality assurance framework for vocational and tertiary qualifications. This framework underpins the entire post-secondary education sector in Australia. If this doesn't interest you, or you're not likely to provide certified training to adults in Australia, you can skip over these next few pages and go straight to the section 'Does an outcome have to start with a verb?'.

What do AQF levels refer to?

If you are delivering certified training to adults in Australia, you may be wondering, *Are the levels of thinking in Bloom's taxonomy the same as the AQF levels?*

Yes and no! In Australia, qualifications exist at the following AQF levels:

- Certificate I
- Certificate II
- Certificate III
- Certificate IV.

According to the AQF website:

> AQF levels and the AQF levels criteria are an indication of the relative complexity and/or depth of achievement and the autonomy required to demonstrate that achievement. AQF level 1 has the lowest complexity and AQF level 10 has the highest complexity.
>
> The AQF level summaries are statements of the typical achievement of graduates who have been awarded a qualification at a certain level in the AQF.

For much more detail on the AQF levels, go to the AQF website (www.aqf.edu.au) and select 'AQF levels and criteria' from the drop-down menu under The Framework tab.

The following table includes excerpts from AQF levels 2, 3 and 4, including the skills and application of knowledge and skills information (my emphasis added). Which levels of Bloom's taxonomy do you think each level roughly translates to? (*Hint:* It's not a perfect fit – one level of Bloom's taxonomy does not equal one level of AQF.)

Skills and their application at different AQF levels

	Skills	Application of knowledge and skills
Level 2	• Undertake <u>defined</u> **activities** • Provide solutions to a <u>limited range</u> of **predictable problems**	Demonstrate autonomy and **limited judgement** in <u>structured and stable contexts</u> and within *narrow parameters*.
Level 3	• Complete routine **activities** • Provide and transmit solutions to **predictable and sometimes unpredictable problems**	Demonstrate autonomy and **judgement** and to take **limited responsibility** in <u>known and stable contexts</u> within *established parameters*.
Level 4	• Complete <u>routine and non-routine</u> **activities** • Provide and transmit solutions to <u>a variety of</u> **predictable and sometimes unpredictable problems**	Demonstrate autonomy, **judgement and limited responsibility** in <u>known or changing contexts</u> and within *established parameters*.

Can you see how the levels build on one another?
- Level 2 restricts the level of thinking to situations that are 'predictable', 'stable' and 'structured', which would indicate Bloom's level 3: APPLICATION at most.
- Level 3 goes up a level, introducing 'responsibility' in sometimes 'unpredictable problems'. This would indicate that Bloom's level 4: ANALYSIS is involved – in other words, having to make decisions based on a number of different factors.
- Level 4 is similar, but introduces 'non-routine' activities, in a 'variety' of sometimes 'unpredictable problems', in 'changing contexts'. This would still be at Bloom's level 4: ANALYSIS, but at the higher end of that level.

> Whether you're using the AQF or not, when creating outcomes for your courses it's imperative that you consider what level of thinking you're expecting your learners to demonstrate their knowledge at – otherwise, your tasks or assessments will be open to interpretation, and this isn't helpful for you or your learners!

Does an outcome have to start with a verb?

Usually outcomes are much clearer when they start with a verb, but they don't have to. You can write outcomes in an 'active' or 'passive' voice.

> I've provided some examples in the following table that come from a communications technician qualification. Which outcomes do you think are easier to interpret?

Example outcomes in active and passive voice

Active voice	Passive voice
Identify system features and control functions	System features and control functions **are identified**
Determine impact of battery and signal levels on system's capability	Impact of battery and signal levels on system's capability **is determined**
Set up mobile equipment to optimise communication	Mobile equipment **is set up** to optimise communication
Select appropriate channels for the communication required	Channels **are selected** appropriate to the communication as required

Whether you write your outcome statements in the passive or the active voice doesn't alter the meaning. The way to choose which way to write your outcomes depends more on what makes more sense to your learners (what appears more natural and easy to interpret), or what is standard in your industry.

Writing outcomes isn't always easy and does take practice, but once you get it right, you're on a clear path to success with and for your learners.

If you're still not convinced about the power of the outcome, consider this story from when I was working in the Pacific islands in Kiribati, as the Senior ESL Education Manager. My job was to increase the level of English being used in classrooms at the college so that the students would be eligible to graduate with AQF-certified qualifications in their trades, in English. Why was this important? If we couldn't prove that 80 per cent of their classes were being taught in English, the certificates would clearly state that the recipient studied in the Kiribati language rather than English. This meant that if they tried to use that certificate abroad, an employer would be unlikely to take them on, preferring to select a candidate trained in English who could communicate effectively with customers and colleagues.

A bit of necessary backstory here is that Kiribati is likely to be one of the first countries with an entire population of environmental refugees due to sea levels rising. The islands aren't in danger of 'sinking' per se; however, once the ground water becomes brackish, the coconut trees won't survive. When that happens, the people will lose their primary source of construction and boat building materials, medicine, food and copra exports. Unless some sort of environmental or engineering miracle occurs, they will be forced to move elsewhere.

The president of the country at the time had requested assistance from the Australian government, which had resulted in the vocational college development program I was employed on. His vision was that if the next generation of children could be educated to an internationally recognised level, they would more likely be able to 'emigrate with dignity', securing well-paid jobs as immigrants, rather than ending up as refugees on welfare in whichever country would take them when the inevitable emigration wave happened. A noble vision indeed!

I was faced with the task of implementing and maintaining an English-only policy throughout the college, which the lecturers delighted in telling me had failed every time it had been tried before.

The strategy had been to give 'fines' to anyone found speaking in the Kiribati language, which meant that students were fearful of being around the lecturers and the lecturers themselves had to enforce this punitive system (which they were reticent about doing).

So I asked them why the kids didn't want to speak in English in the first place. Here's how the conversation went:

Lecturer: If they make mistakes, they'll get mocked by their classmates.
Maria: Mocked? What does that mean?
Lecturer: It's part of our culture – if you fall over, if your shoes don't match, if you say something stupid, we laugh at each other and it's the way we keep each other in line.
Maria: Okay, so mocking is part of your culture, and we don't want to discourage your culture, so how do we get around that?
Lecturer: You can't. Kids will always mock each other if they make mistakes in English, so they won't even try because they don't want to be laughed at.
Maria: Okay, fair enough. I get it. Could we create a 'no mocking of English' rule at the college then? Instead of an 'English-only policy'? Could that work?
Lecturer: Maybe? But I don't think the students will buy it.
Maria: Do they know *why* we want them to speak in English, though? Do they get why the president has pushed for this entire program?
Lecturer: No, but this is just like all the other programs – you lot come in and tell us what to do, then you leave and we drop the whole program because the next lot of foreigners will tell us to do something different.

To be fair, I could understand where they were coming from. We then had a long chat about the president's vision and their children's and grandchildren's futures, and realised that the students likely had no idea about any of these things. They just saw the English-only policy as another stupid rule that came with the foreigners.

So we set up a focus group for those with already quite good English, the student leaders in the college. We talked to them about what the outcomes of speaking English would be for their own futures, and also for the future of their families – including their kids and grandkids – one day. Those conversations turned into discussions we ended up having in each of the classrooms (led by the student leaders and the lecturers). These discussions went along the following lines:

- What happens when the sea levels rise? *We have to move countries.*
- What will happen when you have to move to a new country? *We will have to start everything again.*
- Do you want to **EARN** good money? **MAKE** friends? **BUY** a house and **OWN** a car? **TRAVEL** to see your family and other Kiribati friends? What do you need to **GET** to be able to do all these things? *Good jobs!*
- Will you be able to **GET a good job** if you don't **SPEAK English**? *Probably not.*
- How about your children? And their children? What do you want for them? The same? You will be the first generation of the Kiribati population to lead your families through this big change of moving countries – what life do you want to **CREATE**?

Instead of issuing fines or other punitive measures, we came up with the slogan 'Your future, your choice' – which the student leaders and lecturers would yell out if they heard the Kiribati language being spoken in class. Consequently, the level of English spoken in the college rose so dramatically that the organisation employed to test this every six months declared their latest round of testing invalid because the results were so drastically improved. They believed a 'leak' with the testing materials must have occurred.

On their return to redo the testing – with incredibly tight security in place – they found that English levels had, in fact, improved dramatically, and not because of a security leak. The head of this organisation, who had developed the test 40 years previously, admitted he did not think that improvement on this scale was even possible. He asked us, 'What did you *do*?'

This is the power of showing your learners what outcomes they can achieve. Doing so takes away the barriers and focuses learners on what they'll be able to *do* differently. When you've got a clear outcome to work towards, studying, learning and practising has so much more meaning and is so much more motivating.

If we were able to turn a whole college around by doing this, imagine what's possible by delivering on outcomes-based promises in your courses!

Involve the learner in 'safe space' practice

Ready to have a go yourself? Consider the following outcome – what's wrong with it?

> Understand what to do in the event of an emergency.

Have a think about what this actually means in practice, before attempting the activity provided. The performance criteria listed are at different levels of thinking – can you match them to the right level?

Consider the following levels of thinking:

- **Remember information:** Show us you remember key information.
- **Demonstrate comprehension:** Show us *why* you know it's the correct answer.
- **Apply knowledge:** Respond appropriately in a practical situation.

 Have a go at allocating the different levels of thinking before checking the answers that follow!

1. Explain which fire extinguisher is used for what types of fire.
2. Choose the right fire extinguisher when put in a scenario that involves a fire.
3. Locate the fire extinguishers on a map.
4. In a simulated fire emergency, locate the fire warden and follow their orders.
5. Explain which fire exit you should use in an emergency and why.
6. Locate the correct fire exit for people inside a building that is on fire.
7. Identify the fire warden.
8. Label the fire exits on a building.
9. Describe what the fire warden and everyone else should do in a fire.

Answers:
- **Remember information:** Statements 3, 7, 8.
- **Demonstrate comprehension:** Statements 1, 5, 9.
- **Apply knowledge:** Statements 2, 4, 6.

Practical application – your turn!

Practical task 4: Define the major and minor outcomes of your course and its modules

Not surprisingly, the practical task in this chapter is for you to plan out the outcomes (and practical tasks that guarantee them) in your training.

It's beneficial to have a *major* outcome for the whole course, and *minor* outcomes for each of the sections, lessons or presentations within your course.

For example, what's the major outcome promised in this book? **A universal methodology for how to transfer knowledge with extraordinary outcomes.** The following table outlines the minor outcomes for chapters 1 to 3.

Minor outcomes and the activities that guarantee them

What are the minor outcomes of chapters 1 to 3?	What activities guarantee the outcomes?
1. Create personalised, needs-based training solutions	Task 1a: Create a learner profiling tool
	Task 1b: Expand your activity type profile
2. Set clear expectations of the learning experience	Task 2a: Checklist for presentation outlines
	Task 2b: Checklist for course outlines
3. Implement the 'test-teach-test' paradigm	Task 3a: Integrate standard test-teach-test activities
	Task 3b: Use test-teach-test strategies

Over to you – focus on at least one module of the course you're delivering:
- What's the major outcome of your training?
- What are the minor outcomes?
- What activities guarantee the outcomes?

Remember – the level of thinking from Bloom's taxonomy is less important than every module of learning having a practical task that guarantees the outcome you're promising, and those tasks building on each other in terms of knowledge acquisition and skills development. If you're stuck on using the word 'understand' in your outcomes, flick back to the figure showing Bloom's taxonomy, and the many different learning verbs, earlier in this chapter.

Key takeaways

Well-crafted learning outcomes lead to more effective teaching, better learner engagement and clear evidence of achievement. The key takeaways are as follows:

- Outcome-based learning is essential. With no clear goal, learner motivation and engagement drop. Creating outcome-based modules provides clear direction and purpose.
- Focus on what learners will achieve (outcomes) rather than just listing topics to cover or information to present.
- Five characteristics of good outcomes is that they:
  - focus on what learners can *do* with knowledge
  - form the basis for assessment/evidence of competence
  - use strong verbs
  - target specific levels of thinking
  - avoid the use of the verb 'understand'.
- Connect activities to outcomes. Every outcome needs a corresponding activity that allows learners to demonstrate achievement of that outcome.
- Real learning is application. Real learning happens beyond mere memorisation, when learners can comprehend and apply knowledge in practical situations.

Chapter 4 reflection

Check your answers to the initial pre-test (stage 2 diagnostic) – how much have you learnt? What are your biggest takeaways from this chapter? What will you do differently?

CHAPTER 5

Structure your lessons for success

The outcome

Structure your lessons for success

The why

Why is it important to structure your lessons so they are 'scaffolded' (provided in sequenced, interactive bite-size pieces)?

Quite simply, because you don't want your learners to feel like this poor guy.

At some point in our student lives, we've all been given impossibly long passages of reading to decipher, or been subjected to a never-ending mindless lecture – with the expectation that we'd 'learn' something.

Who stays engaged in that sort of learning experience?

If you don't know how to effectively scaffold the learning experience, your learners won't stay engaged, your attendance and completion rates will be low, and you definitely won't be getting raving reviews.

What happens when you *do* deliberately scaffold the learning journey?

Not only are you building on their previous knowledge, you're building the complexity of the activities from lower to higher order thinking skills, which creates a structure to your training that genuinely piques and holds the learner's interest.

Scaffolding is not just about putting modules or lessons in the right order. It's also about understanding how adults learn, and building their confidence one activity at a time so that they know how to achieve the tasks that will guarantee the outcomes you've promised them.

> **The mind is not a vessel that needs filling, but wood that needs igniting.**
> Plutarch

Have you ever asked yourself these questions?
- How much content is too much content?
- How much should I include?
- Have I given them enough?

The reason you're asking these things is because you don't want to bombard your learners, overwhelm them or ill-prepare them. These are common fears when developing training programs and, fortunately, a simple structure is available that makes it easy to work out exactly how much to include.

At the core of this practical, outcomes-based structure are nine key elements. These are the structural elements I recommend including in every lesson, and this chapter provides demonstrations and explanations of why each element is so important to a well-balanced lesson. If you look back through this chapter, you'll see I've already done the first two, and the following pre-test incorporates the third one. As much as possible, each chapter in this book follows this structure so that, by the end of the book, you'll have experienced it for yourself as a learner. Then it's up to you to decide which elements you'd like to incorporate into your own lessons. (If you want a sneak peek at all nine key elements, go to the practical task at the end of the chapter, or check your answers to the stage 2 diagnostic!)

Pre-test – do you really need this chapter?

The skills check and knowledge check for this chapter are in the stage 2 diagnostic on the Resources page on my website.

The 'what, when and how' (the theory)

What's the strategy that underpins all nine elements?

The test-teach-test paradigm, which I've already provided a whole chapter about. If you can't remember what test-teach-test means and why it's important, go back and quickly review chapter 3, because it's key to creating an engaging lesson structure that works.

Now let's go through each of the nine elements systematically.

1. Promise an outcome (which learners will achieve by the end of the lesson)

The previous chapter in this book was dedicated to why and how to do this. I won't bore you with a recap!

2. Begin the lesson with the 'why', 'WIIFM' or the 'pain–gain motivator'

All these terms mean the same thing, which is 'What's in it for me (WIIFM)?'

For learners to want to learn something new, they need to know *why* it's important, what they're going to *gain* or what kind of *pain* it's going to cause them if they don't engage with the training.

Think about the critical reasons your learners *need* to know what they're learning. What safety issues could arise if they don't learn how to do it correctly? Whose lives could they be putting in danger? How much time/money/effort/resources could they waste doing it the wrong way? How might they humiliate or hurt themselves?

Usually the *pains* are something to do with a loss of time, money, effort or something they consider valuable. The *gains* are the opposites. You don't have to focus on both *pains* and *gains*, but it's always stronger motivation when learners can see both sides.

I've never seen a clearer example of why this is so important than the time I was teaching a bunch of business men in Japan in the early 2000s. They had fairly basic levels of English and were learning so they could interact with international colleagues. In one lesson, we were talking about international politics, and one of the learners piped up with this question, to which I could *not* keep a straight face: 'Maria, do you know, when is George Bush next erection?'

I smiled, then laughed, and then said, 'Okay, everyone repeat after me: eLEction'. To which the entire class chimed back, 'eREction'. We tried another few times but it was the same response. Native Japanese speakers often have trouble pronouncing the 'L' sound because it doesn't exist in their language, so they default to the closest sound they know, which is the 'R' sound. Making the 'L' sound forces you to flick the tip of your tongue against the roof of your mouth, which is actually quite difficult to do if you've never needed to do it before.

I immediately knew that they were never going to realise the importance of getting this word right until they realised what they were saying, so I wrote 'erection' and 'election' on the board, and asked them if they knew what the difference was. They all looked at me with blank stares so I asked them to get out their dictionaries, look up both words, and tell me which one belonged in the political question: 'When is George Bush's next _____'.

They were collectively *mortified* and I've never seen a bunch of grown men try so hard to retrain their mouths to be able to pronounce the L sound correctly. The situation was hilarious for me, but not so much for them – and it was obviously imperative for them as international business men to not get this wrong. This shows the power of really understanding a pain point, huh?

'Pain' and 'gain' statements are usually tailored to the demographic you're targeting – so, for example, if you were trying to 'sell' a weight-loss program to mums in their 40s, you might not focus on how many hours they'll need to spend in the gym. Instead, you could explain the pains and the gains associated with losing weight in the following ways:

- **Pain:** Are you sick and tired of not being able to run around with your kids? Are you annoyed that you don't fit into all those beautiful clothes in your wardrobe anymore? Embarrassed that you're puffed after one flight of stairs? Constantly feeling guilty that you're not looking after yourself and worried that you'll end up with a lifestyle disease?
- **Gain:** How nice would it be to run around with your kids again? To wear all those clothes? To climb a flight of stairs and not be breathless? To feel proud that you're doing everything you can to live a long healthy life?

Sure, that might make sense in terms of Marketing 101, but is it the same inside a lesson? Yep, it's exactly the same.

Let's say the first module in that weight-loss course was about the importance of balancing your macros (doesn't sound very exciting, does it?). So what *would* make it 'exciting' or 'appealing' to someone trying to lose weight? You could start off the lesson by asking which of the following learners would prefer:

- To be confident that you are choosing to eat the right foods in proportions that promote weight loss.
- To be confused by all the different theories (low-carb, high-protein, all-protein, vegan, gluten-free, intermittent fasting) and continue unknowingly making food choices that are actually hindering all your weight-loss efforts.

I know which option I'd prefer! Those are some pretty convincing reasons to learn about balancing macros, right? Promote weight loss, or hinder it – to anyone wanting to lose weight, it's a no-brainer!

CHAPTER 5: Structure your lessons for success ■ 97

It's the same with any lesson or course. If learners know *why* they're about to spend their precious time engaging with your lesson, they're more likely to pay attention and stay engaged. If they don't think much is in it for them, they're more likely to get distracted, not pay attention or not even engage with the lesson at all.

So how do you create WIIFM statements?

Much like I've done in the preceding examples, you need to come up with a compelling reason for *why* it's important for them to learn. You need to demonstrate what they stand to gain and what they stand to lose.

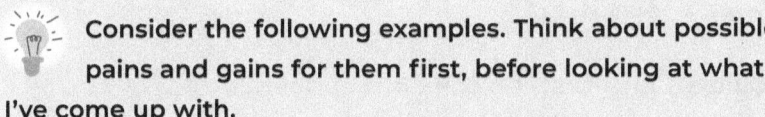

Consider the following examples. Think about possible pains and gains for them first, before looking at what I've come up with.

How would you 'sell' a lesson on the following?
- **Accounting:** Identifying what business expenses you can and can't claim.
- **Carpentry:** Preparing wood before machining.
- **Security:** Restraining a disorderly member of the public.

Here are my ideas:
- **Accounting:** Identifying what business expenses you can and can't claim.
    - **Pain:** If you get audited and you're claiming things you shouldn't be, you could face big fines. If you're not claiming things you could be claiming, you're also throwing money away.
    - **Gain:** Save money, and reduce fines and the stress of being exposed if you get audited.
- **Carpentry:** Preparing wood before machining.
    - **Pain:** Not preparing wood properly can ruin the whole piece of finished furniture that you've spent days creating.
    - **Gain:** Be confident you're not wasting any time, energy or resources, and trust that the end product will turn out well.

- **Security:** Restraining a disorderly member of the public.
  - **Pain:** If you don't restrain the person properly, you could be fined for assault and could also injure yourself, them and innocent bystanders.
  - **Gain:** Have the confidence to de-escalate a situation quickly and safely without risk to yourself or others.

Focusing on both the pains and the gains works well, because always focusing on the negatives can feel a bit 'doomsday' – no-one likes to be 'sold to' with fear-based marketing! Make sure the 'gain' is aligned to what your target audience is aiming for so it's less 'fear-based' and more 'let's succeed in this way for this reason!' Most learners prefer the carrot to the stick.

3. Provide a 'pre-test' on the core concepts

This is a core way of implementing the test-teach-test paradigm; see how confident learners are answering questions about the core concepts *before* your lesson so they're motivated to engage (or skim on past if they don't think they need it). That's the whole point of the diagnostic and pre-test sections in this book. I've been through this concept a lot already so let's move on to the next one.

4. Explain the theory: How much of the 'what & how' do you need?

Theoretical concepts always need to be delivered in any book, course or training program. It can't all be practical, hands-on activities, but it also doesn't have to all be lecture or reading style either.

If you stick to the structure recommended in this chapter, you should only include enough theory and demonstration so that learners are able to do the practical tasks without too much difficulty.

So how do you present that theory and demonstration, without it just being reams of text on screen or hours of lecture? We started exploring options for this in the first chapter of this book, including all the ways you can engage the various learning styles and multiple intelligences (such as visual, tactile, audio, social, spatial and logical).

Regardless of whether you're delivering training online, face to face or in a blended format, you can present information in images, text, video, or slide-based presentations. Alternatively, you can lead learners on a discovery learning exercise to find answers from a completely different source, manual or textbook.

If you're holding live group sessions (online or face to face), you can also ask learners to teach each other with 'reading gap' or 'peer teaching' activities. This is where learners are put into small groups to first learn about a piece of the theory, and then split up into groups with learners from the other groups so they can all teach each other about what they've just learnt.

It's all about getting learners to interact with the content as much as possible. Whole programs are available that can teach you how to 'gamify' learning, but in this section I'm just going to briefly show you the kinds of activities that will help you transform traditional lecturing or reading based activities into interactive discovery based learning activities.

While you're reading – think about which of these you could replicate in your presentations or courses.

5. Demonstrate with clear examples

I've created an entire resource book – *The Engagement ToolKit* – that covers how to transform a lecture-style monologue into collaborative, communicative activities that get learners engaged and thinking. The goal of all of these activities is to get your learners interacting with the concepts and helping each other learn, instead of you doing all the 'teaching' – remember the old adage that 'the best way to learn is to teach!'

This resource book is available on the Resources page on my website in the Introduction section, and I'd recommend reading up on these activities if you're not already familiar with the following concepts:
- flip cards – to present questions and answers or key words and definitions
- 'categorise this' – to match key concepts with definitions or examples
- using charts or tables – to piece together missing information.

Let's take these three activity concepts and see how they could be applied to teaching a lasagne recipe.

Now you could just get learners to read and then follow the recipe. That's a bit boring, though, isn't it? How about, instead, you:

- Use flip cards:
  - On one side, write the ingredient.
  - On the other side, write the quantity.
  - Ask learners to quiz each other on what they think the quantities would be to feed a family of four.
- Get learners to categorise:
  - Write out a list of recommendations and ask learners to work out whether they're true or false (for example, adding sugar to the sauce, using only beef mince, or adding three layers of bechamel sauce).
  - Debate the concepts with learners, discussing why they think they're right or wrong.
- Create a table:
  - Either on the board or in a worksheet, create a table that looks like the one provided but blank out the answers (the grey shaded text in the table here).
  - Ask learners to brainstorm what they think the answers are, and then discuss the answers so they can fill in the blanks, or give them cards with the greyed-out information and then debate which cards they think go into which spaces.

Example table showing not recommended and recommended actions

	Not recommended	Recommended
Adding sugar, salt and spices to the sauce	Adding sugar to the sauce	Adding salt and spices to the sauce
Pre-cooking lasagne sheets	Pre-cooking the lasagne sheets	Adding the lasagne sheets directly from the box onto the meat sauce layers

CHAPTER 5: Structure your lessons for success ■ 101

	Not recommended	Recommended
Number of layers of Bechamel sauce	Adding two to three layers of bechamel sauce	Adding only one layer of bechamel sauce as the last full layer before the final sprinkling of cheese
Type of mince to use	Using only beef mince	Using a combination of pork and beef mince

Isn't this table far more powerful than reading or listening to the recommendations in a paragraph like the following?

> We recommend that you don't add sugar to the sauce, and instead add only salt and spices. We also don't recommend pre-cooking the lasagne sheets; rather, just add the lasagne sheets directly from the box onto the meat sauce layers. Adding two to three layers of bechamel can be a bit rich so we recommend only adding one layer of bechamel sauce as the last full layer before the final sprinkling of cheese. Only using beef mince can be quite heavy so we recommend using a combination of pork and beef mince.

Theory can be dry, forgettable and tedious. It's your job to break it up into interactive, bite-size pieces that your learner can relate to – ask as many questions as you can to get them *thinking* and *digesting* information, rather than just attempting to *absorb* information through a continuous firehose!

> **What's most important is that learners grasp enough of the *theory* and see enough *examples* of it in action so they are well-prepared to do the *practical tasks* that will achieve the *outcome* you've promised. No more, no less.**

Why is demonstrating more important than explaining?
Along with getting enough *theory*, learners need to see several *examples* for the theory to really 'land'. Have a look through the previous pages in this chapter – every time I introduce a concept, I provide a few different examples so you can see the concepts in action.

The problem with not giving enough clear examples is that people can only interpret what they see, hear or experience based on their background experience and knowledge.

Let's take a food example. If you said 'good food', your learners could interpret that as anything from an organic beef hamburger on sourdough to a gluten-free vegan burger. Similarly 'good food' could be interpreted as the food you get from a 'hole in the wall' pop-up, or from a five-star fine-dining degustation.

Before sending learners off on a practical task or assessment, provide worked examples so your learners can *see* the standard that is required of them. If possible, provide a few different examples so they can see the scope of possibility or ways the task can be completed.

Assessments or practical tasks shouldn't be a guessing game for learners – they should have clear instructions and demonstrations so they know exactly what standard they need to produce to be deemed competent or pass the assessment.

Remember the writing outcomes example from the previous chapter, where I walked you through all the different ways you could write outcomes at different levels based on 'understand what healthy food is'? That's a perfect example of a worked example of a practical task. Before asking you to write your own outcomes, I wrote out a series of outcomes at different levels as examples, so you could see the differences between the levels of thinking.

I've included worked examples in every chapter of this book, and because I do like to practise what I preach, I'm going to demonstrate this concept in a different way, thereby giving you a second example of why giving solid examples is so important.

Fancy playing a game with me? Go on, it'll be fun – promise!

> Right. Imagine you're learning a foreign language and I'm your teacher. I put this image in front of you and tell you the word for it is *zuzu*.
>
>
>
> - What do you think the English word for it is? Just go with your first answer. Don't think about it too hard.
> - Right. Now say *zuzu* 20 times while looking at it.
> - Got it? Understood? Right. Now I'm going to test you on it.
> - What's the English word for *zuzu*?
> - If you said 'a circle', or 'a dot', you're wrong.
> - How are you feeling?
> - I hope you enjoyed your learning experience, and I hope you come back for the next lesson and rave about my teaching skills.
>
> Errrr, no. Clearly not. Unfortunately, this is what a lot of learning experiences feel like.
>
> Theory, theory, theory, with little explanation, demonstration or chance to test your knowledge out. By the way, how stupid did you feel saying a word 20 times assuming you knew what it was, and then being told (more than likely) that you were *wrong*? Did you feel a bit stupid? Sadly, this is how a lot of learners feel when they don't get enough demonstration or theory, and then – *bam* – are expected to test their knowledge or ability to apply the concept in real life. They feel stupid,

a bit vulnerable and, quite frankly, not enticed to come back for another round of humiliation. It's like being firehosed with information in a lecture, and the lecturer then pointing at you and asking you to explain what they've just said – *eww*! An awful experience for everyone involved.

So let's leave that in the dust, and see what giving proper examples can do for the user experience.

Play the game again with me, but let's do it properly this time.

Imagine you're learning a foreign language. I put this image in front of you and tell you the word for it is *zuzu*.

- What do you think the English word for it is? Just go with your first answer. Don't think about it too hard.
- Did I hear you say 'a circle'? Well, it is a circle, but it could be other things too. Can you think of other English words that would describe that image?
- You might be thinking, *dot*, *full stop*, *ball*, or anything from your life experience. Well, all those things could be right, but what if I showed you the following examples? What do they and the image above all have in common?
    - The first televisions only showed pictures that were white and _____.
    - The raised keys on a piano are _____.
    - The colour of bitumen is _____.
    - The type of magic used by witches can be called '_____ magic'.
- What's the English word for *zuzu* now? (Did you just go 'Ahhhhhhhhh'?)

> - If you said 'black', you're right! Hoorah! *Zuzu* means black in English!
> - Now. Can you find something immediately that's *zuzu*? Hold it up and say *zuzu*! Then point to something else that is *zuzu*, and say it again! (If you're really playing along, you're now holding or pointing at black things).
>
> And immediately *you* the learner knows you've nailed it, and as the facilitator, I know it too.

Tada! How are you feeling after *that* learning experience?

Better than the first round? I hope so! Everyone will interpret your 'theory' differently, depending on their perspective, experience and background. I dive into this concept more in chapter 9, when I cover how to build rapport and not alienate your learners. For now, what's most important to remember is that it's *your* job as the facilitator to ensure that everyone gets a chance to interpret the information in the way you were intending them to. You'll only know that you've done that successfully if you follow the recommended steps of explaining first and demonstrating thoroughly next.

The more examples you can provide – good, bad, ugly, right, wrong, competent not yet competent – the better!

You cannot transmit wisdom and insight to another person. The seed is already there. A good teacher touches the seed, allowing it to wake up, to sprout, and to grow.

Thich Nhat Hanh

6. Involve the learner in 'safe-space' practice: What do you need to consider about involving the learner in activities and assessment tasks?

Certain aspects of practice tasks need to be considered before you expect to assess your learners or send them out to use these new skills in the real world.

Knowing what theory to provide is one thing. Knowing what examples or demonstrations to give is another. Your learners being able to translate all of that into achieving the outcome is something else entirely. What really helps learners achieve outcomes is involving them in practice activities where they're confident to have a go, knowing they're 'safe' from harsh judgement, ridicule or punishment.

Consider these questions for your own teaching and learning scenario:

- How many times do learners see you demonstrate the task before being expected to try it themselves?
- Do you discuss the process as you're demonstrating? Can you get your learners to describe the process as you're doing it, explaining why each step is important and what they must remember *not* to do?
- What level of supervision is required? Is peer-supervision appropriate? At what point?
- In what setting will your learners be able to practise these tasks? In private? In front of colleagues? Only with you as their trainer?
- Is there a benefit to practising tasks in groups and learning from each other's mistakes?
- How can you provide a 'safe' practising environment for your learners? Not just physically, but also so a level of trust and willingness to 'have a go' exists, even if they don't get it right the first time?

These questions have no right or wrong answers – every training program and learner present different scenarios. The answer to the last question is essentially about building enough rapport with your learners that they trust you can provide that safe space.

I learnt the power of doing that out in the Pacific. Remember the story right at the beginning of this book about the senior teacher who was so stuck in his ways I called his bluff and told him he could leave the program if he just tried this new idea once? If not, go back and have a read. It's the perfect example of building enough rapport with your learners that they have the courage and confidence to give something new a red-hot go – and surprise themselves by succeeding!

7. Provide a practical task: What do you need to keep in mind about assessing learners, or helping them to achieve the outcome you promised?

I could include another whole chapter on assessment, but considering why you're likely reading this book (to become better at transferring your knowledge), I've decided that's not the best use of our time. If you do need to assess your learners formally (in the Australian Qualifications Framework, for example), or provide evidence for accreditation or licensing requirements, you will need to follow the assessment procedures and guidelines that are set out by your organisation.

Having said that, here are a few FAQs I get around quizzing and testing learners in both online and face-to-face learning environments.

- **Do I really need quizzes or tests at the end of each module? Can't I just test learners at the end of the course?** The more opportunities you provide for learners to test their knowledge, the easier it is for you to pinpoint where the gaps in learning may be. If you wait until the end, you're missing out on opportunities to isolate where learners are struggling – and to help them address it before they move on. I'm sure you've been in courses where you've missed some foundational knowledge from an earlier module that has then been to your detriment as you've gone through the rest of the course. Avoid this scenario at all costs – test learners throughout the course and address gaps in knowledge or understanding before they become bigger problems down the track.
- **Should I provide the answers to quiz or test questions?** Yes! This allows learners to learn from their mistakes or challenge their existing knowledge as they're going through the course. The only time I don't recommend providing the answers is if it's the final assessment, and 'passing' that assessment should be straightforward if

they've 'passed' all previous mini assessments. If they then fail the final assessment, they will need to go back through and review their mini assessments before attempting the test again, which can only be a positive reinforcement for their learning. Also providing the answers for the final assessment can encourage cheating or passing on answers to other students, which completely defeats the purpose of having a final assessment.

- **What's the difference between formative and summative assessment, and do I need both?** Formative assessment is when you're collecting evidence throughout the course that the learners are building their knowledge and skills – perhaps through informal quizzes, reflective writing pieces, collaborative assignments and/or journals. Summative assessment is when some kind of final exam or assessment proves learners have achieved the outcomes or competencies they set out to achieve at the start of the course. Of course, someone can 'flunk' a final assessment for many reasons, even if they do have the knowledge and skills. So my recommendation is usually to have a mix of both types of assessment. If you have to choose between them, I'd always err on the formative side rather than the summative. Why? Formative assessments show you how a learner has progressed over time, while summative assessments are literally just a snapshot of how they were able to perform on a given day. How would you prefer to be assessed?

8. Summarise key learnings

It's always good to wrap up a lesson with a summary of what they've learnt. If possible, get your learners to do this instead of spoonfeeding them (unless time is an issue, of course!). Ask your learners about their biggest takeaways from the lesson, so they can verbalise or write it down in their own words. When we write things down, we're more likely to remember – that's why note-taking is so effective!

Recapping at the end is often quite surprising for them (due to how much they've learnt), especially when they have their original thoughts to compare it to.

You know how in every chapter I ask you why you think the chapter topic important and how you are already implementing it into your classroom? How do you feel when you get to the end of the chapter and I ask you to think about how much you've learnt and what you can implement into your own teaching practice in the practical activities? Do you feel a sense of accomplishment on some level?

I'd hope so! That's exactly what you'd want for your own learners too, right?

9. Provide a core concepts quiz
This is the final chance for your learners to check how much they've learnt. If the core concepts quiz is provided as part of the pre-test and then again at the end of the lesson, learners can also literally quantify how much they've learnt by comparing their right and wrong answers for both versions of the quiz. This can give a great sense of achievement to the learners, and also serve as an indicator of how effective your lesson has really been. Double bonus! If several learners are still getting particular core concept quiz questions wrong at the end of the lesson, it can be a good indication of an area of your lesson that needs to be improved.

Practical application – your turn!

Do you think there's room for improvement in your course and lesson structure? Not surprisingly, the practical task here is to plan out how you could implement all the elements of a best-practice adult learning lesson.

Practical task 5: Structure a lesson plan

How would you take the elements we've been through in this chapter, and adapt an existing lesson plan to include them? Create a document with these sections. (I personally use Google Sheets, but a Word doc, Canva doc or Excel doc will do the same thing.)

Go through your lesson and summarise the following:
1. Outcome
2. The why
3. Pre-test
4. Theory
5. Demonstration or example

6. Safe-space practice
7. Practical task
8. Summary
9. Core concepts quiz

Every chapter in this book follows this structure. I've put a sample lesson plan template on the Resources page on my website – simply navigate to the chapter 5 resources to access.

Once you can do this for one lesson, you can systematically apply this structure to all of your lessons until you have a comprehensive course overview. Documents like this can help you systemise and sell your expertise, or standardise your curriculum against industry standards – which is the content of the next chapter!

Key takeaways

Whether you're teaching art, accounting or acrobatics doesn't matter. Find out how much your learners know first, so you don't end up teaching them things they already know. Then give your learners enough:

- reasons to *motivate* them to *want* to learn it
- theory to help them understand *how* to do it
- examples that *show* it done 'properly' right through to 'poorly' (so they can see for themselves all the different ways it can be done and learn how to avoid mistakes)
- activities that create a safe space to help them practise how to apply their new knowledge and skills in the real world.

Depending on the situation, you might also like to test learners before and after, summarise the key takeaways like I'm doing now, and provide a final reflection activity. Funny that – here's one of those coming up next.

> **Chapter 5 reflection**
>
> Check your answers to the initial pre-test (stage 2 diagnostic) – how much have you learnt? What are your biggest takeaways from this chapter? What will you do differently?

CHAPTER 6

Systemise, consolidate and leverage your expertise

The outcome

Systemise, consolidate and leverage your expertise

The why

Why would you want to do this?

This chapter is all about the power of a well-structured curriculum map. Curriculum maps apply if you're a subject-matter expert (SME) in the business of selling products and services based on your intellectual property (IP), or if you're in an organisational learning and development (L&D) or HR role that requires you to map out your curriculum against industry standards or for internal auditing processes.

If you're in the L&D role and you're familiar with curriculum maps and how to use them to map learning pathways and ensure a course is comprehensively aligned with the requirements of your organisation or industry, use this chapter as a refresher or a confirmation that you're on the right track, or a challenge to see how you could enhance what you're already doing.

If you're an SME, you more than likely have an enormous amount of IP in your head, or scattered across various folders, which you've created for different clients over the years. If you've decided to evolve your methods from a one-to-one model of teaching into a one-to-many model, having a curriculum map – or a summarised overview of your content – will help with that process. Systemising your IP with the formula I present in this chapter makes creating multiple learning products from that same set of IP much easier. You can create free and paid versions of learning products that all serve different purposes: one-on-one, group, live, evergreen, online or face-to-face learning products such as books, diagnostic surveys, webinars, podcasts, keynotes or courses.

Hang on, what is a curriculum map?

If you're unfamiliar with the term 'curriculum map', they look like the following example, which is the one that I created while writing this book. Sometimes they're called different names depending on the organisation but, regardless of the name, they provide an overview of your learning content and practical tasks or assessments. What's important to note is that these maps are different for every situation: the columns that you include in curriculum maps will vary depending on the needs of your organisation or business.

Example curriculum map

	Pain Points	Gain Points	Outcome	Theory	Case Studies / Examples	Practical Activities
1.1	Alienate with learners, make learning harder, pitch too low or high, humiliate yourself and your learners	Connect with learners and build rapport and trusted relationships where learners are confident to achieve success	Create personalised needs based learning experiences	--Questions to ask learners (ed background, personal goals, barriers to learning, learning styles) --Benefits of asking questions --Catering to all learning styles --Activity types for different learning styles --Learning needs surveys (precourse survey and 'getting to know you' activities, online and offline)	--Refugee - what is my home country? --Afghani interpreters culture shock --Fidgety learner --TAFE lecturers intercultural non-understanding --Japanese girl behaviour - non-verbal --How I am 3 different learning types in 3 different scenarios	1.1.1 Create Learner Profiling Tool 1.1.2 Activity Type Profile
1.2	Learners lose faith in you, get disengaged, feel duped, give bad reviews	Learners gain respect for you, can withdraw if not in the right course and know exactly what they paid for and will achieve	Set clear expectations of the learning experience	Presentations & Courses / Events: What expectations should you cover before starting? --Content and outcomes --Equipment and tools required --Delivery mode and expected involvement --Communication and support --Assessment and feedback	--Disorganised trainer not giving assessment guidelines until week 7 of a 12 week course --Course outline vs intro module --No assessment criteria = A and D grades in different units	1.2.1 Checklist for Presentation Outline 1.2.2 Checklist for Course Outline
1.3	Learners get bored, demotivated, disruptive, passive involvement, firehouse with too much information	Active participation, making learners think, motivated to learn more, question, think and discover	Implement the Test-Teach-Test paradigm	'Test-Teach-Test' paradigm ways to implement: --reflective activities --make titles questions --create activities that make the learner brainstorm answers --remove strategic parts of the learning content --provide questions before offering a reading, listening or watching activity --apps --workbooks Types of Activities: Reflection, Comprehension, Application	Sewing machine service example - questions before content	1.3.1 Integrate standard Test-Teach-Test Activities 1.3.2 Use Test-Teach-Test Strategies

If you're in an L&D or HR role in a large organisation and need to map professional learning pathways for your employees, your organisation may use different terms for, firstly, a series of courses and the order in which they need to be taken by various cohorts, and, secondly, the mapping process of a singular course.

No standard approach to mapping curriculum exists, and some institutions even use this term to describe how to choose the units that must be completed in a degree program (as opposed to the granular nature of showing the theory, assessments and alignment to industry standards of each unit).

It really is a very individual exercise, so keep that in mind when I'm taking you through the rest of this chapter.

Pre-test – do you really need this chapter?

The skills check and knowledge check for this chapter are in the stage 2 diagnostic on the Resources page on my website.

Explain the 'what, when and how' (the theory)

What is the purpose of a curriculum map?

If you're a university organisation mapping the engineering curriculum, for example, you could have curriculum maps that show the theory and assessment tasks for each unit in each of the semesters that don't look dissimilar to my map just provided. Additional columns may also show how the units relate to the engineering standards in Australia, or whole other maps that show how the units comply with industry-based competency frameworks that are required by law if a graduate of the program is to be awarded with that qualification. An example of such a map can be found on the website for the University of New South Wales. Go to www.teaching.unsw.edu.au/curriculum-mapping

and look at Example 5 under the 'Examples and types of curriculum mapping at UNSW' options.

Such details may be required legally to prove that the entire program is fair, equitable and includes all necessary components as required by the university, the national qualifications framework and all appropriate industry standards.

Columns such as 'pain points' and 'gain points' might not be required, and 'outcomes' may be called 'objectives'; the terminology will depend on your specific situation.

If you're an SME and want to use the curriculum map to extract different learning products from your IP, you will want to include the pain and gain columns (for marketing content – more on that later), but you may not need to worry about columns that align your content with industry standards – or perhaps you do!

Every organisation will have different requirements. Check out www.teaching.unsw.edu.au/curriculum-mapping for a comprehensive overview of what is required in the University of New South Wales curriculum maps. You can also access different examples and types of curriculum mapping at UNSW, and see the myriad different types required just by one university.

Regardless of all of these variations, the core purpose of a curriculum map is to be able to see your whole course, or a series of courses, from an 'eagle view'. Doing this enables you to assess where the gaps are, whether the modules are sequenced correctly and where possible repetition may be, and to ensure that the entire course is balanced in terms of theoretical content, practical tasks and assessments.

So, what's the process for getting your IP systemised into a curriculum map?

If you're working in L&D in an organisation, you'll likely already have access to a curriculum map or overview of all your training courses. If not, or if you're an SME with content that has been created for various clients and is scattered all over your hard drives, I have a clear process for you to follow. In short, you need to:

- **Commit to the process:** This is the hardest part! Bring all the IP into one folder – all the different versions, all the worksheets and slides, the lot. I know this is hard, but if you don't do it thoroughly, you risk missing core content.
- **Do a brain dump:** This is an extension of the lesson planning task in the previous chapter, except now you're doing it for all of your modules, using all the IP you gathered in the previous step.
- **Systemise the IP:** Now you need to populate that curriculum map from the lesson planning brain dumps. Some people find it easier to work in columns (completing categories such as all the activities, and then all the theoretical points), while others prefer working by the rows (completing a full module at a time before moving onto the next one). It's really up to you and how your brain is wired. Do what feels easiest!
- **Extract products and build offerings from the map:** Once your curriculum map is populated, you'll be able to use what's in the columns in different ways, as shown in the following table.

Building content from your curriculum map

Section	Learning products	Content	Example
The pain/gain points	Articles, blogs and podcasts	All the 'before' and 'after' success stories, and how you came to learn the lessons you learned can become motivational content that helps build trust with your learners and helps them to see the benefit of engaging with your content.	'Would you prefer to be the presenter who sends everyone to sleep, or the type of presenter who has the audience laughing, asking questions and thanking you with an enthusiastic round of applause?'

CHAPTER 6: Systemise, consolidate and leverage your expertise ■ 117

Section	Learning products	Content	Example
The outcomes	Quizzes, surveys and diagnostic tools	Outcomes are all the things you're promising your learners will be able to 'do' – so create a survey that asks about their current level of confidence in each of those items. If they score low, they know the module is right for them! This is especially helpful for training that is for inductions or compliance based, where the initial motivation to engage may not be that high.	'How confident are you giving an engaging presentation? Which of the following strategies are you already using? Rate yourself on a scale of 1 to 10 – with 1 being not confident and 10 being confident – for each of the strategies. If you score less than x, you might find this course is right for you!'
The theory + case studies	Books, presentations or online courses	This is the core content that underpins the whole topic. A book could contain one chapter per topic, for example, explain all the theory and then show detailed case studies that demonstrate the theory.	Chapter 1: Using animated slides – why, how, and some good and bad examples. Chapter 2: Using images rather than text – why, how, and some good and bad examples
The practical activities	Workshops or one-to-one coaching sessions	This is where it all comes together – the practical activities are usually reserved for offerings that provide support, such as coaching sessions or workshops. However, you can provide 'self-study' versions of all practical tasks – learners just won't receive feedback. I've done this at the end of each chapter in this book!	

What other learning products can you provide?

Whether you're an L&D professional or an SME, all of the elements in the preceding table (pain/gain points, outcomes, theory and activities) would be part of the most baseline learning product you can provide. This is commonly called an 'evergreen' or 'self-study' version of your course.

You can create 'higher touch' products by adding on other services. Think of this as being like 'nesting' your learning products, as shown in the following figure. Add a 'community' element to it (through a Teams, WhatsApp or private social media group), or create a time-limited 'intensive' group study version (starting and finishing at designated times), with one-to-one or group support from a mentor or facilitator. The 'workshop' level adds a face-to-face element, and the 'mastermind' level involves all of the workshop elements stretched over a longer period – for example, six months or a year – and can also include VIP options such as 'think tank' days or retreats.

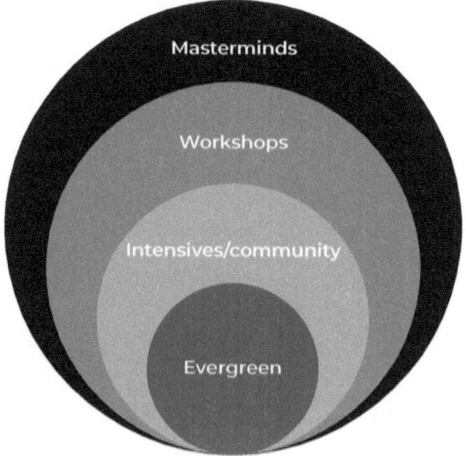

Creating 'higher touch' product by adding other learning services

How do you choose which learning products to offer?

Good question. I learnt this the hard way, by creating a range of products and services and then running myself into the ground trying to deliver them all. Where did I go wrong? I wasn't operating in my zone of genius, and I wasn't doing things that I loved. I succumbed to the hype, and tried to do what everyone else was doing – namely, a bunch of online options that just never really felt right. #TrustYourGut

CHAPTER 6: Systemise, consolidate and leverage your expertise ■ 119

So instead of trying to simultaneously write articles, do presentations, offer online tutorials, manage two Facebook groups, run online free to the public '12 Day Challenges' and a twice yearly e-course (after also doing consulting work, taking on coaching clients and running a small business), I've made my offerings much simpler now.

I do the things that light me up:
- I write, including articles, stories and lessons with stories. I love writing and it's something I can spend hours buried in.
- I deliver keynotes and workshops to audiences in boardrooms and ballrooms – because I absolutely *love* delivering live training, and harnessing the energy of a room full of people.
- I produce best-practice lessons for other organisations, and help their SMEs deliver face-to-face training more effectively.
- I coach motivated professionals to create their own learning materials.
- I do some consulting on aid and development projects, spending time working on location, with local stakeholders offshore.
- I take on the role of 'project manager' when my clients don't have capacity.

No longer do I stretch myself trying to deliver group programs or live, online courses, because my ideal clients don't want or need that kind of learning experience. They come to me because they need the skill set I've just described. Simple, right?

> **Offer what your learners need *and* what you're happiest delivering – your learners will pick up on it if you don't.**

Perhaps you're an SME, however, and you've got more questions like:
- Should you stick to one learning product, or is having multiple best?
- How do you choose which learning product to create first?

Here's a process to help you figure out which learning products suit you and your ideal learners the best. This process is based on the following figure, which you can use without even reading the content if you'd prefer not to do more reading!

Working out which learning products to deliver

Which learning products can you deliver?

Mode	Self-Study				Group Study			Personalised	
Purpose	Access information at any time, self-paced learning, no group or community				Receive feedback, work in a team and demonstrate competence			Receive personalised action plan and/or outputs, project management	
Product	Opt-In	Books or Interviews	Evergreen Course	Library	Community	Workshop	Licenced Course	Session	Report or Output
	Quiz, Blueprint, How to Mini-book, Challenge, Promotion & Marketing Materials	Discussions or Interviews, written or recorded on audio	Modules with action points	Many modules in different areas	Place where people can communicate	Experiencing modules with group of learners	Course delivered to train trainers	One to one, face to face, solutions created during 'session'	Problem presented, research completed and solution provided
Online Mode		e-Book or Podcasts	e-Course	e-Library	Forum, Facebook Group	Challenge, Intensive e-Course,	Intensive e-Course, Mastermind	Via phone, or video conferencing	
Offline Mode		Book	Presentation + Worksheets	Library	Meeting, Gathering	Workshop, Mastermind	Facilitator Manual	Session Notes, Feedback	Report, Output
What role are you playing?	1) Determine whether the client is the right fit	1) Provide self-access information, curation, workbooks, videos, transcripts, podcasts.			1) Provide materials that are studied in groups, with accountability, discussions and/or dedicated timelines. 2) Work with learners to achieve quantifiable outcomes. 3) Engage the group of learners to interact with the information and with each other to enhance the learning experience.			1) Work with a client on achieving a specific goal. 2) Provide strategy, personal support, and accountability.	1) Work for a client on achieving a specific goal. 2) Provide services as requested to achieve the specific goal outputs
		Author, Lecturer			Facilitator of Learning, Teacher or Trainer			Coach	Consultant

Task 1: What roles do you want to play?

What role are you playing?	1) Determine whether the client is the right fit	1) Provide self-access information, curation, workbooks, videos, transcripts, podcasts.	1) Provide materials that are studied in groups, with accountability, discussions and/or dedicated timelines. 2) Work with learners to achieve quantifiable outcomes. 3) Engage the group of learners to interact with the information and with each other to enhance the learning experience.	1) Work with a client on achieving a specific goal. 2) Provide strategy, personal support, and accountability.	1) Work for a client on achieving a specific goal. 2) Provide services as requested to achieve the specific goal outputs
		Author, Lecturer	Facilitator of Learning, Teacher or Trainer	Coach	Consultant

Ask yourself:
- Do you have colleagues or a team who can help with the authoring or facilitating?
- How big is your team and what HR do you have who can be part of the content-creation process?
- What's the best use of your time, and what do you want to invest your time into creating?

Task 2: What modes are best for you and your clients?

Mode	Self-Study	Group Study	Personalised
Purpose	Access information at any time, self-paced learning, no group or community	Receive feedback, work in a team and demonstrate competence	Receive personalised action plan and/or outputs, project management

Then decide:
- What modes your products would be best suited to in terms of the needs of your learners: self, group or personalised study options?
- Do your learners need 'one-to-one' support?
- Would they be better supported in a group?

Remember – unless you're providing mandated training, engagement is always far higher when support is offered.

Task 3: What products are best suited to your target learners?

Product	Opt-In	Books or Interviews	Evergreen Course	Library	Community	Workshop	Licenced Course	Session	Report or Output
	Quiz, Blueprint, How to Mini-book, Challenge, Promotion & Marketing Materials	Discussions or Interviews, written or recorded on audio	Modules with action points	Many modules in different areas	Place where people can communicate	Experiencing modules with group of learners	Course delivered to train trainers	One to one, face to face, solutions created during 'session'	Problem presented, research completed and solution provided
Online Mode		e-Book or Podcasts	e-Course	e-Library	Forum, Facebook Group	Challenge, Intensive e-Course,	Intensive e-Course, Mastermind	Via phone, or video conferencing	
Offline Mode		Book	Presentation + Worksheets	Library	Meeting, Gathering	Workshop, Mastermind	Facilitator Manual	Session Notes, Feedback	Report, Output

Lastly, decide which products are best suited to your learners. Sometimes this can be tricky if you have various groups of learners with different needs (staff training is different to educating the general public, for example).

The most important question you need to ask yourself here is what do your learners actually want?

If you don't know, you need to ask. After a year of struggling to deliver a suite of learning products and services, I rang 70 of my preferred clients and asked them what they actually wanted. Their answers blew me away, because it was the opposite of what I was expecting. They didn't want an online course, a community, a membership or a library of resources – they wanted my brain on their project, focused, private, one to one.

Well, didn't that simplify my offerings (and life) overnight?!

You might be equally surprised if you haven't yet polled your target learners – so do this first and save yourself the time and energy involved with creating something none of your learners are interested in!

The other question I'm often asked is which version of a course to create first: 'one to one', group face to face, or the online self-study version. Most people would intuitively think creating the online self-study version first is easier, but in my experience the 'one to one' and live group versions really help you identify what works and what doesn't. Once you've got those offerings working, you can extract the self-study version.

Practical application – your turn!

Practical task 6a: Curriculum map

Create your own curriculum map using the instructions in this chapter. You don't need a template; you just need a document where you can create a bunch of columns and rows. I prefer Google Sheets so if you do want to start with my template, you can download it from the Resources page on my website. Remember, though – what columns you need to include are completely up to you and what your organisation or business needs to see mapped out.

At a bare minimum, include the following five columns:

Pain/gain	Outcome	Theory	Demonstration	Activity

Practical task 6b: Learning product plan

Thinking about your base IP, decide which learning products you are most likely to extract. Which ones make most sense to focus on creating first? Choose from:
- articles, blogs and podcasts
- quizzes, surveys and diagnostic tools
- books, presentations or online courses.

What levels of service can you provide for your learners? Remember – if you don't know what your learners would prefer, ask them first! Consider:
- workshops or one-to-one coaching sessions
- community
- intensive group study version or workshop
- mastermind programs, including 'think tank' days or retreats.

If you find these two tasks hard, remember that you're not alone! Professionals often struggle to do these two tasks alone because, although they're SMEs, they're not necessarily language or learning experts. If you need assistance, find a curriculum developer or education specialist who can help!

Key takeaways

Systemising and consolidating your expertise allows you to provide a comprehensive overview of the depth and quality of the experience that your courses provide. The key takeaways from this chapter are as follows:

The process for systemising and consolidating your expertise is, in summary:
- committing to the process by gathering all your intellectual property

- doing a brain dump of pain points, outcomes, theory, examples, and practical activities for each module or unit
- organising your knowledge into a curriculum map
- extracting various learning products.

Your IP can be repurposed into different learning products:
- pain points → articles, blogs, podcasts
- outcomes → quizzes, surveys, diagnostic tools
- theory + case studies → books, online course content
- everything including practical activities → workshops, one-on-one coaching.

> **Chapter 6 reflection**
>
> Check your answers to the initial pre-test (stage 2 diagnostic) – how much have you learnt? What are your biggest takeaways from this chapter? What will you do differently?

Where to now?

Now that you've built a solid connection with your learners, and created lessons that are well-structured, comprehensive and free of repetition, you need to move on to creating learning resources that communicate clearly with your learners. All the connection and structure in the world won't help if your slides are set up to turn you back into a lecturing machine! This is where the design and delivery of your learning materials are important. Well-designed visual aids are great – until they're not delivered well! This next stage will show you how to do both, in ways that will transform ordinary learning experiences into ones that are extraordinary.

OUTCOME: Build and deliver engaging learning materials that motivate your learner to succeed

STAGE 3

COMMUNICATE: Resources development and delivery

Once you know you're addressing the needs of your learners and that your lessons have a solid structure, it's time to address the way you *communicate*. This is not about communicating *at* your learners, but about communicating *with* them – engaging learners is about opening up two-way conversations, rather than saturating them with monologues. It's about motivating them to want to get involved, making them think, engaging them in the process of learning, asking questions, and building on their existing knowledge.

I'm not just talking about 'death by PowerPoint' slide decks here, either – whether it's slides, worksheets, online lessons, videos or step-by-step tutorials, the way the learning materials or resources are designed and delivered, and so the way they communicate with your learners, matters.

Real learning occurs when learners can apply their new knowledge in the real world. Throwing a bunch of theory at them and hoping they 'get it' is old school, and most of it goes in one ear and out the other, anyway. Would you prefer to be lectured at or actively involved in the learning experience? Would you prefer to leave the classroom scratching your head wondering whether you did, in fact, understand, or leave knowing you've nailed it because you've just spent the latter part of the lesson practising and getting it right?

How well do your learning resources support the learner to apply their new skills and knowledge in the real world?

If you really want to *communicate* effectively with your learners, you need to:

- choose a user-friendly delivery style that maintains currency
- provide powerful visual aids to assist in discovery-based learning
- use techniques to build rapport and maximise engagement.

And, yes, these topics are covered in the next three chapters. If you're pretty sure you've got this stage covered already, confirm it by doing the stage 3 diagnostic on the Resources page on my website. (Scan the QR code to access.)

If you do 'score' highly, I'd still recommend skimming through the chapters, just to confirm you're on the right track.

CHAPTER 7

Choose a user-friendly delivery style that maintains currency

The outcome

Choose a user-friendly delivery style that maintains currency

The why

Why is it important to have a user-friendly delivery style?

Because when you don't, your learners are highly likely to end up frustrated, bored or waving the white flag and giving up altogether.

User experience (UX) is *everything*. Think about that app you've downloaded and abandoned because the interface was not intuitive and left you going around in circles. Remember that online shopping experience that did not result in a sale because the website made it too hard to find exactly what you were looking for? Think about those face-to-face shopping experiences that have left you walking out the door because the sales staff were either too pushy or nowhere to be found. That app, website or bricks and mortar store won't be high on your list of places to return, but the places that *will* be high on that list are the ones that made it easy for you to get what you were looking for.

Whether or not you return for more comes down to how you, the user, felt trying to be part of that experience; if it worked for you and was joyful to be a part of, you'll go back for seconds. If not, you probably won't, unless you absolutely have no other choice.

It's the same when creating learning experiences. When the user is at the centre of your learning development process, you can engineer a learning experience that is tailored to their needs. Deliver learning in a way that makes your learners feel like they're part of the process and getting exactly what they need, and they'll keep coming back. If they feel alienated or intimidated, they more than likely won't come back, will be resentful of having to attend or will disengage.

If you're actively facilitating learning (as opposed to supervising), three main delivery styles can be applied to any lesson. There's a time and place for all three styles and sometimes you can use all three styles in the same class; it depends on the outcomes you're hoping to achieve with your learners.

The three main delivery styles are as follows:

1. lecture style
2. discussion-based learning
3. problem-based learning.

They all have different purposes, levels of 'scripting' required and various 'preparation' levels.

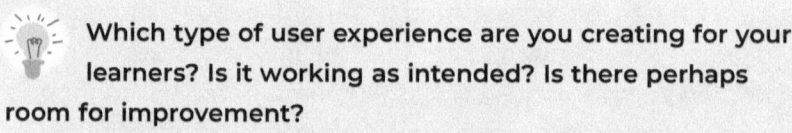

Which type of user experience are you creating for your learners? Is it working as intended? Is there perhaps room for improvement?

Regardless of the delivery style, your lessons should also abide by copyright conventions and maintain their currency.

Why is this important?

Because you don't want your materials to date, if at all possible, and you don't want to be in contravention of the laws surrounding intellectual property. You wouldn't want your materials used without your permission, so I'm assuming you'd like to extend the same courtesy to other SMEs!

Regarding currency, when things change, you want to be able to update your learning resources as quickly as possible, or even better, not have to update them at all because of the way you've engineered them. Either way you'll save yourself time and your learners the angst of discovering too late that your materials aren't up to date (or the last minute scramble to update before you present! Yeah, that's not me, I've never done that.... pfffft! Who hasn't?).

Learning never exhausts the mind.

Leonardo da Vinci

Pre-test - do you really need this chapter?
The skills check and knowledge check for this chapter are in the stage 3 diagnostic on the Resources page on my website.

The 'what, when and how' (the theory)
What does user-friendly delivery sound like?
Essentially, this whole book is about creating a learning experience that is engaging and involves the learner, rather than just providing information for them to read or watch. How do you make the whole experience user-friendly, though?

You need to consider the 'tone' you're using. This comes back to the question I posed back in chapter 3. Do you want to come across as a lecturer who is firehosing your learners with information? Or do you want to come across as a facilitator who is leading them on a guided learning journey?

If you want to achieve the latter, my advice is to *have a conversation with them*, don't just throw information at them. See, I'm doing it now ... asking questions, giving answers, interacting like I would if I were talking to you face to face.

Now, of course, this is easier to do when you are delivering face to face, but the same principle applies for any kind of learning experience that involves reading, watching or listening tasks.

We've entered a new age. Formal, stuffy language is a feature of a bygone era when it comes to communication – be it on television, on social media, and even in marketing and learning experiences.

I was recently working with a large government organisation on their online courses, and after honing and refining the language so it was more conversational and spoke directly to the learners (rather than using the standard formal corporate tone), I was told the course didn't sound professional enough and we needed to remove all the questions and conversational-type language. At the end of the day, the client got what the client wanted, but not without gentle protest from me. Just because you're in a corporate environment, does that mean you can't communicate in a way that is user-friendly? Think about that conundrum for a moment: what would you prefer as a learner in a corporate environment?

I've got a whole heap of examples coming up that demonstrate how communication has evolved and how you can apply it to your own learning resources, but before we get to that, I've got a very simple question for you to ponder for a few moments.

When you're teaching or presenting, what's your tone?

What kind of learning experience are you creating for your learners? One-way 'lecture' style, or a two-way 'conversation style'? Stuffy corporate or user-friendly?

Demonstrate with clear examples

Not convinced a 'conversation-style' tone is appropriate for your learners? It might not be! Before you make that decision, though, put yourself in the learner chair for a moment.

CHAPTER 7: Choose a user-friendly delivery style that maintains currency ■ 133

> 💡 The following information has been presented in two ways. Read through both options and decide which is more engaging. Which option would you prefer if you were given the choice? Read them out as if you were teaching the content in front of a live audience – which learning experience, audio or text-based, would you prefer to be the learner in?

Option 1: Lecture style

Social media has changed the way we communicate during 'one-way' exchanges. Advertising 30 years ago and advertising today are very different. Newspaper articles in the '90s and online news these days are also very different. Current affairs programs have changed from being 'reporter' style to being discussion-based. This completely different way of communicating has affected the way we communicate across many different mediums. The tone has become much more direct, relaxed and conversational – and there's no reason the way you present online learning should be any different, because this is what people expect these days.

A fine line exists between lecturing and providing solid information your learners can engage with. The trap with online learning is to cut and paste long 'chunks' of information you know your learners need to digest, to create reading or listening activities (like this one). The art of making it engaging is to break it up and make it speak directly to learners, by employing lots of different techniques – such as using bullets, giving demonstrations, asking questions and breaking it up into paragraphs that answer questions they may have as learners (the opposite of what I'm doing here).

You don't have to be as 'relaxed' or 'informal' as I'm being in this passage – your choice of tone all depends on your learners and what level of professionalism and formality they're expecting from you and the learning experience.

Option 2: Conversation style

How has social media changed the way we communicate during 'one-way' exchanges?
Well, consider advertising 30 years ago and advertising today. Think about how formal the language was in newspaper articles in the '90s, compared to how informal online news is these days. Ponder that for a second ...

Could you imagine a current affairs program like *The Project* being aired 30 years ago? Traditionally, current affairs programs were journalists in suits, ties and high-collar blouses performing serious interviews with harsh lighting (think Jana Wendt on *60 minutes* in the 80s, if you're Australian). These days? It's very different, isn't it?

Is it just the formality and level of 'seriousness' that has changed?
No. Don't you think the tone has become much more direct, relaxed and conversational as well? Again, think about a program such as *The Project*; even its headline highlighted that they were there to 'dissect and digest the daily news, events and hottest topics'. The show included discussion, laughter and banter between the hosts, much like there might be around a dinner table discussion. If you watched the show, did you often end up continuing the conversation long after the show had ended?

Current affairs has become something to 'discuss' and 'dissect', rather than something to 'report'. Old-style programs like *60 Minutes*, launched in 1979 in Australia, are based on a 'reporting' style of delivering information, as demonstrated in their headline: 'Join television's top reporters as they investigate, analyse and uncover the issues affecting all Australians'.

What's the link between social media and online learning?
Communication has changed – there are no two ways about it. Lecturing is an old style of delivering information. It's the

60 Minutes of the online learning world and if you're delivering information this way, you're going to lose your learners. Think about the audience that *60 Minutes* attracts. (*Hint:* It's not millennials.)

How do you change a 'lecture' into a conversation?
Don't fall into the trap! It's easy to cut and paste long 'chunks' of information as a reading or listening activity. Instead:
- Break it up!
- Ask lots of questions.
- Use bolding to make the questions stand out.
- Mix up the formatting.
- Use bullets.
- Demonstrate (like I'm doing here) instead of just explaining.

Does this mean you have to stop being professional?
No! Of course not! You don't have to be as 'relaxed' or 'informal' as I'm being in this section – your choice of tone all depends on your learners and what level of professionalism and formality they're expecting from you and the learning experience.

Which option was easier to engage with? Option 1 or 2?

I don't know about you, but I'd choose option 2 hands down, every time. Option 2 involves you as the learner – asking you questions, giving answers and challenging what you already are thinking.

If ABC News and the BBC can do it, so can you. I've included links to two articles on the Resources page of my website, under the tab for this chapter. The first article is from ABC News and is about camels being disqualified in a beauty competition for using botox (yes, really), and the other is a more serious piece from the BBC about what happens after the Pope dies. The task here is to recognise how news stories these days, be they serious or a bit of fun, use a more conversational tone, punctuated by bolded questions that keep you reading. If you want a challenge, see how many examples like these you can find in the wild!

The 'what, when and how' (the theory) continued ...

The delivery styles we're about to discuss lend themselves to a more conversational style of learning but, first, let's consider scripts and whether they're good to have on hand when delivering.

Are scripts advisable when it comes to teaching and learning?

Scripts are good for situations where you need to

- remember every detail in exact order, including word choice, and keep to exact time limits
- concentrate in a professional, high-pressure situation where you have distinct corporate responsibilities to deliver a certain message in a certain way (think post-emergency government response).

Rarely do these situations occur in the types of ongoing face-to-face learning environments that most of us are faced with as subject-matter experts (SMEs) working with people who are there to learn from our knowledge and skills.

Scripts can also be helpful if you're looking to create a robust online learning module. From a solid script, you can create highly engaging online modules of learning, assessment tasks and reflective activities; however, you'd never present a script in its entirety for learners to read from top to bottom. How to turn a script into a guided learning experience complete with self-assessment tasks is a whole other book. #WatchThisSpace. Or, follow closely how AI tools are developing as they can now do almost the entire job for you!

Is there anything wrong with reading from a script?

Yes, and no. It all depends on how comfortable you are with the content and how comfortable you are reading from a script. Unless you're practised, though, it can sound a little robotic.

If you're trying to connect with your learners and engage them in the learning experience, having a script can be beneficial to keep you on track, but reading directly from it rarely enhances the user experience. Think about the lectures or presentations you've sat through where someone is clearly reading from a script. It's rarely what you'd describe as inspiring or entertaining, right?

If you really need to use a script, read it to yourself so many times that the content rolls off your tongue easily. If you want to sound natural, inviting and engaging, reading it word for word will not get you there. Practise it over and over until you're so comfortable that the script is really just a reminder; most of the words are already committed to memory and you know exactly when to pause and add emphasis. You also know the content well enough that you're comfortable to make little side jokes or go off script a little bit. This way, you can deliver it with warmth and honesty and you'll sound way more natural and believable.

There's definitely a time and place for scripts but they don't really work in an outcomes-based classroom.

How do you encourage a more 'conversational-style' tone in your delivery?

I'm assuming you'd prefer to sound 'conversational' rather than deliver content 'lecture style'. Encouraging more conversation in your learning experiences is all about creating more space for 'discovery-based learning'.

The next chapters in this stage outline how to create slides and other visual aids that assist in the discovery learning process but, for now, let's just briefly touch on how to encourage a more 'conversational' style when you're presenting off a slide or image-based presentation.

A lot of presenters choose to put the majority of their notes onto the slide and then proceed to read that content (sometimes almost verbatim) to their audience. Cue 'death by PowerPoint'.

Here's an alternative (and the first recommendation I always make when a professional asks me to help them improve their presentation):

- **Slides:**
    - As often as possible, start with a question as the title of the slide.
    - Reduce the amount of content so you're not tempted to 'read' it off the slide – change bullet points to key words only so you're forced to describe, demonstrate or explain the core points, or ask learners to brainstorm and provide answers.

- **Presenter notes:**
    - Put your extended notes into the 'notes' section of the PowerPoint (or onto palm cards if that makes you more comfortable).
    - Write notes in note or bullet form, not full sentences, again so you're not tempted to read from them line by line.

The idea with these recommendations is that you're encouraging a conversation, rather than a lecture. Your presenter notes are not intended to be read *from*, but to read *through* if you need a reminder or a memory jog.

Also, putting questions on the slides gives your learners time to *think*, involves them in a question-and-answer type interaction and also gives *you* time to refresh your memory if needed – before you open the floor for the group to discuss the answers. This is another iteration of the test-teach-test paradigm already explored in chapter 3.

Creating discussion points for the learners, providing key word hints for them to consider the answers and ensuring you have good notes to refer to helps you to:
- remember all the points you want to deliver in the lesson (you should be familiar enough with the content so that key words are enough to jog your memory on what needs to be covered)
- calm your nerves (all the information is there, so you can't forget it!)
- not overwhelm the learners with all the details (goodbye 'death by PowerPoint').

No-one can possibly remember every point they need to deliver. That's what your presenter notes are for. More tips on how to sound more engaging and natural are coming up next but, for now, let's focus on the type of delivery style you can use.

What do the different styles mean?

Here are some basic definitions:
- **Lecture-style learning:** The facilitator delivers theory or information via a monologue that learners listen to.

- **Discussion-based learning:** The facilitator asks a series of questions, and a series of parallel activities are provided so learners can discover the content via shared discussions.
- **Problem-based learning:** The facilitator gives the class (or small groups) a problem or series of problems to solve. Learners solve the problems and then deliver the solutions to other learners via short monologues, explanations or demonstrations.

What style is best?

Trick question! That question has no simple answer. The styles all serve different purposes and have their place in a classroom at different times.

It's kind of like a wardrobe – you likely have different styles for different occasions. If you're hoping to relax and kick the footy around, you don't use your best suit. Choosing a delivery style is kind of the same.

So when is it best to use each style? It depends on what you're hoping to achieve in the lesson. The question you need to ask yourself is, 'What's the purpose of the lesson?'

Purpose 1: You need to get a bunch of theory out to students

A lecture-style delivery can be suitable if you're delivering to a large group, or you have to deliver the lesson in a flipped style (pre-recorded). Generally speaking, standing at the front of the classroom and delivering hours of monologue is neither engaging nor interesting.

Alternative: You can still deliver theory, but in a much more engaging way, by using discussion-based learning techniques. For example, instead of lecturing chunks of content, try the following:

- Set readings for homework, with a series of questions that learners can be prepared to discuss during the next lesson. They're reading instead of listening to you deliver, and the core questions and answers can then be discussed as a group. This is far more interactive and engaging than simply listening, taking notes and hoping to absorb the knowledge, right?
- Adapt this idea to the in-class version by posing the same questions to the whole group and getting learners to read very small chunks of the theory silently in class, before deciding on what the

answers should be with their peers. Once small groups have confirmed their answers, discuss the questions and all possible answers as described in the preceding activity.

> ### Demonstrate with clear examples
> Say you were going to deliver a lecture to a group of psychologists on the top five ways to assist women in their 50s after being diagnosed with ADHD. Instead of lecturing for an hour, provide a written version of the theory and ask learners to read it silently. (Remember – most people can skim read much faster than the same text can be read out loud). Ask them to rank the five ways to assist women from 'most helpful for my clients' to 'least likely to recommend for my clients', with rationales for why they're ranked in that order.
>
> The psychologists could do the reading task for homework, or you could split the class into five mini sessions where learners read about one way to assist only, before discussing with their peers whether they agreed or disagreed with the recommendation and why it would or wouldn't work for their clients. Either way, it's taking the onus of *you* to lecture (and your learners to sit passively observing), and putting the onus on your learners to discover and discuss the theory and how it applies to their own lives.

Problem-based learning can also be suitable for delivering theory, if the core materials/textbooks provide the solutions. Again, you can assign a 'problem' that learners work together in groups to engineer solutions for; you can be on hand to guide the process, point out things they may have missed, or do a brief lecture to the whole group if a theoretical point doesn't seem understood or clear. You could even ask them to solve the problem by asking an AI app such as ChatGPT to come up with a solution for their problem – and then get them to figure out (by using academic or professional resources) whether the advice is sound or not, and why.

These skills of critical thinking, problem-solving and evaluating search engine findings are what today's workplaces need – more than receiving and regurgitating knowledge, no? The days of listening and regurgitating are long gone!

Purpose 2: You need to demonstrate your theory

How can you turn the 'demonstration' part of your lesson into a lecture, a discussion or a problem-solving session?

Of course, you can read out case studies *lecture* style, but you could also make the lesson a little more interesting by giving a case study to each small group and getting them to *discuss* questions in small groups, or come up with solutions for the *problem* that the case study presents.

You could also prepare questions that reinforce main theoretical points, ask your learners to *role-play* different case study scenarios, and then follow up with group *discussions* on how the theory relates to the examples.

Role-plays can also be the basis for *problem-solving* scenarios where learners put their theoretical knowledge to the test, to come up with a *solution* for the unique problems presented by the case studies.

Purpose 3: You want your learners to practise skills

If you want your learners to practise their skills, *lecturing* is not going to get you anywhere. Providing opportunities for practising skills is also a fantastic way to follow up with *discussions* based on what they learnt from the experience.

If a particular hiccup occurred in the practical task, and a learner made a significant error or mistake, this is a great opportunity for a *problem-based* learning experience. Ask the learners to come up with strategies for avoiding and or preventing similar mistakes in the future.

Which styles take the most preparation?

Lecturing does require significant preparation – you need to finalise the structure, main points, examples, demonstrations, compelling introductions and conclusions, scripting and the practising of the script until you're comfortable to deliver without reading verbatim from your slides or palm cards.

Discussion-based learning requires a lot less preparation, but does require thought in terms of the questions you'll be asking and the points/notes/theory you want to ensure have been delivered by the end of the class. The bonus of this style is that often your learners will deliver a lot of the content for you, and all you need to do is guide the lesson in the right direction, rather than deliver all the information yourself, especially if you're getting them to *find* the answers in a textbook or reference book.

Problem-based learning requires even less preparation because, theoretically, you as the SME should *know* the solutions to the problems you're presenting to your learners, and also the problems would normally be everyday issues that you come across in your field of work. Well thought through case studies definitely do take some preparation but, essentially, this type of learning takes the *least* preparation because the onus is on the learner to come up with and workshop solutions with their peers, with the facilitator simply there to guide the process.

There really is no 'right' or 'wrong' with which style you choose, as long as it's not boring the living daylights out of your learners; using all three styles at different points of the lesson is highly recommended.

What's the best way to maintain the currency of your materials?

Do *not* recreate the wheel. Instead, here's what I recommend for online and face-to-face materials:

- Put as many questions as possible, and as few answers as possible, in your workbooks or on your slides. The questions rarely change. The answers might, though. So if your slides are 'answer heavy', you'll need to keep updating them. If your slides are 'question heavy' you will need to update far less.
- For online videos:
  - Have as few long tutorial videos as possible. Break them up into smaller videos so you can edit only the things that change instead of having to re-do the whole video.
  - Change the format of long tutorial style videos into a slideshow option with text, video or audio snippets, attached to each slide. Again, it's easier to update a single slide than having to redo a whole video tutorial.
- Link learners out to external content, instead of embedding it into your own course. That way, the primary source of information will always be up to date.

Imagine a policy document you've referenced right throughout your visual aids is updated. All the page numbers have changed, the pages look different and, therefore, every single slide and page in your materials will need to be updated.

No. Just *no*. Ain't nobody got time for that! Unless you're a masochist, save yourself the time, effort and energy by providing live links out to any document that you reference in your courses, or at the very least provide a downloadable version of that document. If the document changes, all you'll need to do is re-upload the new document – rather than updating all the lessons you've cut and pasted that information into.

What do you need to know about copyright?

Copyright can be an absolute minefield! I discussed these issues with the people who specialise in intellectual property and copyright issues at the Department of Training and Workforce Development (DTWD) in Western Australia, who clarified some of the most common questions course creators ask.

Demonstrate with clear examples

If I wanted to embed a TED Talk from YouTube into a lesson, is that allowed? With appropriate referencing? Or do I need to seek permission from the owners of the video?

According to the experts, it depends on how you're going to use it. Even if you're working for an educational institution, the TED Talk rules are quite specific about *not* allowing the embedding of their talks in commercial projects – that is, if you or the organisation you're working for receives money for the course, you're not allowed to embed it without permission.

In fact, according to the experts at DTWD, 'Section 28 of the Australian Copyright Act allows trainers to freely play or stream third-party content in the classroom but only in very specific non-commercial circumstances'. Surprised? So was I! You can access more information on the TED Talks Usage Policy via the link on the Resources page on my website. (This page also provides information on seeking permission for corporate use.)

> *I know that taking IP from another source and putting it into my lesson without reference or permission is not allowed. Can I make reference to an article, though, and send students out to the website it's hosted on from a link within my course? Do I need permission from the owner to do this?*
>
> Another good question! If you think that you don't need permission in this case, you're mostly correct! Having said that, some websites ask you *not* to link back to their pages, so it's always best to check the terms of use.

What else do you need to know about copyright?

As mentioned, copyright can be a bit of a minefield, so I'm going to practise what I preach by sending you out of this chapter so you can engage with an up-to-date course on this instead! This course is super comprehensive and written by the experts, so me recreating the wheel is pointless.

The 'Copyright – Doing it Right' course is written by experts at Western Australia's DTWD. You access the link on the Resources page on my website. This link takes you directly to the lesson on third-party content, which explains when and how you can use other people's material in your courses.

> **You can't push anyone up the ladder unless he is willing to climb a little himself.**
>
> Andrew Carnegie

What are the best ways to maintain currency and adhere to copyright laws?

Time for action! Make a commitment to keeping your content current and adhering to copyright conventions with the following:

- **How:** *Not* cutting and pasting chunks of information from source documents. If at all possible, link *out* to the documents, ensuring you've received permission from the site or author of the content where appropriate.

- **When:** If you *need* to reference images or facts from the documents, make a commitment to review your materials at least once a year to ensure that the information is still current. Put the date in your diary as a recurring event.
- **Which resources:** At the start of the course, keep a record of the slides, pages or other visual aids that contain information that may need to be updated.
- **Which references:** Also keep a record of any policy/external documents you reference in the course so that in your annual review you can easily check whether the documents have been updated.

Practical application – your turn!

Practical task 7a: Delivery style reflection

Ask yourself these questions to help you consider how you might improve your lessons:

- How 'user-friendly' is the tone and language you use in your learning experiences?
    - Is it on the lecture end of the spectrum? Is it conversational? Have you included lots of questions? Could it be improved?
- What percentage of your presentation is 'scripted'?
    - Where do you keep your 'notes'?
    - How much of a script will you rely on?
    - What do you put on your slides?
- Which delivery styles do you use? Lecture? Discussion? Problem-solving?
    - How could you use more discussion and problem-solving style activities in your lessons to balance the lecture-style parts?

Practical task 7b: Currency and copyright commitment

How are you going to abide by copyright and maintain the currency of your materials across your visual aids, including in your slides, online lessons and in your workbooks?

- Use the recommendations provided in this chapter to plan your commitment to getting this right:
    - How will you create content in the future (or adjust your existing content)?

- How often will you review your content? When is your next review due?
- Which of your slides, workbook pages or other content will need to be reviewed on a regular basis?
- Which external resources or references will need to be reviewed on a regular basis?

Key takeaways

Here are the key takeaways from this chapter:

- User-friendly delivery is crucial. When the learning experience isn't user-friendly, learners can become frustrated or bored, or give up entirely. Good UX (user experience) makes learners want to return.
- Conversational is often better than lecture style. Modern communication has evolved to be more direct, relaxed and conversational. Conversational teaching styles engage learners better than formal lecture styles.
- Mixing delivery styles is recommended. Use all three delivery styles where possible: lecture style, discussion-based and problem-based learning.
- Scripts should be used with caution. While scripts can help keep you on track, reading directly from them can sound robotic and reduce engagement. If using scripts, practise until the content flows naturally.
- Maintain currency of materials. Make slides and workbooks 'question heavy', break long videos into smaller segments for easier updating, link learners out to external content rather than embedding it, and review materials regularly to ensure information remains current.

Chapter 7 reflection

Check your answers to the initial pre-test (stage 3 diagnostic) – how much have you learnt? What are your biggest takeaways from this chapter? What will you do differently?

CHAPTER 8

Provide powerful visual learning aids to assist in discovery-based learning

The outcome

Provide powerful visual learning aids that question, engage and assist in discovery learning

The why

Why is it important to ensure visual aids are structured so that they question, engage and assist in discovery learning?

Technology has made us lazy. PowerPoints were heralded as the be-all and end-all for an engaging presentation but the reality is that a lot of presenters use them as a dumping ground for the entire set of content they wish to deliver. Cue 'death by PowerPoint', bored learners, zero retention of knowledge and little to no engagement. We've also become lazy with 'tick and flick' learning – the type of online learning experiences where you provide scores and scores of text and expect learners to 'learn' from it. Urgh. Yawn.

Death by PowerPoint is not cool

- **Death.**
- **By.**
- **Powerpoint.**
- **IS.**
- **SO.**
- **NOT.**
- **COOL.**

- Join.
- Me.
- In.
- Saving.
- The.
- World.
- From.
- More.
- Pointless.
- Torture.

- Join.
- Me.
- In.
- Creating.
- A.
- New.
- Standard

Tell me you've never been bored out of your mind by slides that were full of way too much information or an exact copy of what the presenter was saying to you. Tell me you've been motivated by 'homework' of reading 300 pages of research articles before turning up to the next lecture but having *no clue* as to what you're reading for, or what sense you're meant to make out of any of it. No doubt you remember thinking, *Why am I reading this? What is the point of this? Why are we learning this? Are we ever going to use this?*

Although structure and delivery styles are also important, well-designed, 'discovery learning' based visual aids really are the key to keeping your learners engaged with the learning process. Nothing is wrong with setting 300 pages of reading material for homework; it's what tasks you set alongside that reading that will make the difference.

It's about making your learners *think*, *do* and *be active* in the learning process. Can visual aids really help you do that? Yes, they can. Think of it like this:

- **Spoonfeeding your learners information** (dumping all the information into a handout, slide or workbook) **= a passive learning experience**. They don't have to *do* anything, because you've handed it all to them. These kinds of learning experiences tend to go in one ear and out the other. Expecting your learners to learn by taking notes while you lecture is about as outdated as lecturing itself.

CHAPTER 8: Provide powerful visual learning aids | 149

- **Well-designed and executed visual aids can create an active learning experience**, by putting your learners in the driver's seat. This allows them to question, think and discover instead of being passive in the learning process.

The easiest way to explain this is by thinking of two ways of delivering a set of five bullet points on a PowerPoint. It could look like either of the slides in the following figures.

The first slide is pretty passive. You just have to read through the text and you have all the information. You don't really have to listen to the lecturer at all but, if you do, you probably will only be hearing half of it because you're also trying to read.

A 'passive' PowerPoint slide

How do you write a
Well-Structured Script?

It's best to provide enough:
- **reasons** to motivate learners to stay engaged throughout the lesson
- **outcomes** so they know what they're aiming to achieve
- **theory** required to grasp the ideas required to fulfil the outcomes
- **examples** of positive (and not so positive) attempts at fulfilling the outcomes
- **activities** for learners to apply their new knowledge so they can achieve the outcomes

Now consider the facilitator putting up the second version of the slide, while also saying, 'So what do you think these terms refer to? Have a quick think before I tell you what I think they mean'.

A slide encouraging a more 'active' learning experience

How do you write a
Well-Structured Script?

Provide:
- reasons
- outcomes
- theory
- examples
- activities

Immediately, you'll be scanning the words, thinking about what you already know, deciding on your own answer, and then waiting to find out whether you're on the right track or not. It's human nature to want to answer questions and to find out whether you're right or wrong.

How much more powerful is the second alternative, rather than just passively listening to someone reading through a set of facts?

This concept doesn't just apply to designing slides; it also applies to all types of visual aids, including workbooks, technical posters or diagrams, handouts, cheat sheets, manuals, textbooks, reference material, flashcards, a whiteboard, sticky notes, realia (real objects such as tools, equipment and machinery) and videos.

What's key here is the concept of 'active learning'

When in doubt, look at your visual aids and consider the way you're using them with your learners. Are they actively making your learners *think*? Are they helping you create opportunities for collaboration, communication and discovery-based learning? If not, ask yourself why you're providing them.

If your answer is 'to provide a summary of what they've learnt', you've essentially just taken part of the learning experience *away* from them. This may sound a little counterintuitive, but consider how much more powerful it is for learners to be involved in creating a summary of what they've learnt, instead of having it handed to them.

Is this chapter all about creating better PowerPoint slides?

No. You can find hundreds of lessons online about how to use PowerPoint effectively, so I didn't think that would be the best use of our time.

Having said that, all of the strategies in this chapter can be applied when using PowerPoint slides. I've also included the criteria I use for assessing slides at the end of this chapter, but we're mostly going to focus on how to use *other* visual aids in your learning spaces.

Most importantly, know that even dry, technical content doesn't have to be dry and boring!

No-one wants to learn from someone who is rambling on, bumbling through their slides and having to check key facts mid-lecture. If you often find yourself rehearsing your lectures word for word, or slipping into 'lecture' mode, using your notes for guidance on every slide, believe me when I say a better way is possible! If you'd like to learn how to run a learning experience that involves more discussion and less explaining, and more fun, collaborative activities rather than awkward one-sided lectures, this chapter is for you.

I've worked on lessons covering everything from microbiology to train driving to accounting, and can tell you the reason lessons tend to be dry and boring is *not* because of the content. It's usually because of the way the visual aids are designed to be delivered.

Creating engaging visual aids isn't rocket science, but when you're aware of the main tips and tricks, you'll never look at a presentation in the same way again – especially if it's someone else's. Ready to critique your own resources first? Find a presentation, a workbook or a learning resource that you use with your learners and keep it in mind when going through the pre-test section that's coming up next.

Pre-test – do you really need this chapter?

The skills check and knowledge check for this chapter are in the stage 3 diagnostic on the Resources page on my website.

The 'what, when and how' (the theory)

How do you create visual aids that aid in the discovery learning process?

The answer to that question lies in the terminology itself. Visual aids are meant to 'aid' your lesson 'visually'. They're not meant to teach your lesson for you.

In the coming sections, I provide alternatives to lecturing from a slide deck, or dumping all your content onto long pages of text. I also talk about several activities that I outline in more detail in *The Engagement ToolKit*, which you access via the Resources page on my website. If you're not familiar with the following activity types, please have a read over them before continuing on:

- think, pair, share
- line races (this might sound like a kids' activity but adults will definitely request this activity if you teach them regularly!)
- peer teaching
- speed dating (yes, you can use this concept in a classroom too, and it's not about meeting a new love interest!).

My personal philosophy is that if you're having fun, you're learning. Games are fun and don't detract from the learning process – if anything, they enhance it! If you're not convinced that getting people out of their seats and moving around is beneficial to the learning process, search up 'action-based learning', or 'the neuroscience of play and learning', and then tell me I'm wrong!

To convince you further, here are some insights into the neuroscience behind play and learning from *Your Brain on Art* by Susan Magsamen and Ivy Ross:

There's a myth that learning is meant to be serious business. When you see a visual of someone 'learning', it's usually a person bent over a book in quiet contemplation. Rarely do you see a photo of someone in the throes of a full belly laugh, head thrown back, eyes watering from laughing so hard. But our brains love humour. Genuine laughter lights up multiple regions of the brain ... electrical signals spark the cerebral cortex into action, and you laugh, which activates the brain's reward system, releasing dopamine, serotonin, and the same kinds of endorphins let loose in response to sex, food, and exercise. Dopamine is vital to learning: it helps with goal-oriented motivation and in the laying down of long-term memory, which is crucial to retention. Humour is a learning juggernaut.

How do you use visual aids (other than PowerPoint) to make learning more fun, interactive and memorable?

Before I give you some ideas, have a think about it yourself – how would you use visual aids in your classroom? Options include the following:
- technical posters, diagrams or images
- manuals, textbooks, handouts, cheat sheets or reference material
- flashcards
- whiteboard
- sticky notes
- realia (including tools, equipment, machinery)
- videos.

Consider whether you could incorporate any of the following ideas into your classrooms moving forward.

Technical posters, diagrams or images

When considering posters, diagrams or images, also consider whether the following could work:
- Provide unlabelled graphics so that learners can test their knowledge before 'discovering' the answers in the reference materials.
- Get learners to create their own 'posters', labelling the parts of a device, or drawing timelines for processes showing key stages.

Consider these two suggestions from another angle. Can you make these activities part of the workbook so learners can take them away? (Remember – learners being part of the summarisation process of core content is far more impactful than simply providing it to them already summarised in a worksheet.)

Here are some further options:
- Use diagrams or graphics in a peer teaching activity, where each small group gets a picture to 'study' together (using the reference materials), before 'presenting' the core concepts to other groups.
- Create a quiz based on information found in a diagram, *before* you present the information (test-teach-test). If they're getting all the answers right, you can turn that lesson into an extension activity rather than lecturing them on things they already know.
- Use diagrams, posters or timelines at the start of a new lesson to quiz or review the previous lesson's work.

Manuals, textbooks, handouts, cheat sheets or reference materials

In much the same way as learners can use diagrams or posters within your lesson, they can also use reference materials to 'discover' the 'answers' instead of you physically explaining it to them.

For example:
- Create a quiz based on 20 pages of their manual, dividing it into four parts.
- Use this quiz as a peer teaching activity, where each group focuses on their part only first. Half the members of each group can then move clockwise to the next group and 'teach' the new group their part, before the new group teaches them their part. Keep moving the groups until everyone's had a chance to be taught the three other sections.
- Instead of a peer teaching activity with the quiz, you could ask each group to present the answers to their part to the rest of the group. This means the learners are essentially teaching each other and you're on hand to guide if points are missed or misunderstood.
- Instead of presenting the answers, each group could ask the rest of the class to guess what they think the answers are, and then guide them with hints until they do get the right answers.

CHAPTER 8: Provide powerful visual learning aids — 155

If you're creating online self-study lessons, you can also send learners to external sources to find answers to the questions you provide in the lesson. You don't need to reinvent the wheel. You can provide questions they search for, and then reveal the answers or provide a quiz so they can test what they've learnt.

> **Remember – using reference materials such as manuals and textbooks should be all about your learners searching for answers, rather than being drowned in information they don't know how to process or what to do with.**

This idea was reinforced for me most recently when I was studying that master's program in Norway. (Despite all the horror stories, the course did offer some wonderful lecturers and learning experiences, believe it or not!) One lecturer loved to give us 800 to 900 pages of reading per week, with absolutely no guidance on what we were actually reading for – more than just for 'general knowledge'. Without a purpose for reading, I found myself skimming through the readings trying to grasp the core concepts instead of reading deeply; when pushed for time, I'd only read the abstracts. Instead being given a task like, 'Compare these three articles and summarise the differences in the way the author tackles the question of *xyz*' would have created a purpose for me to read and understand the articles at an entirely different level.

Moral of the story: give your learners a purpose for reading the reference materials, or don't expect them to process these materials anything deeper than at a surface level.

Liking these ideas? I've got pages and pages of suggestions like these – including using other visual aids such as flashcards, whiteboards, sticky notes, realia and videos to transform a lecture into a collaborative, interactive lesson in which learners are engaged. You can find these ideas in *The Engagement ToolKit* (accessed via the Resources page on my website).

Are workbooks a visual aid as well?

Yes! Workbooks provide an excellent opportunity for your learners to capture core information. Do you remember the three types of activities from chapter 3 you can provide in a workbook? Here they are:

1. **Reflection activities:** To brainstorm prior knowledge or future application.
2. **Comprehension activities:** To record new knowledge and learning content.
3. **Application activities:** To apply new knowledge in real-life scenarios.

How do you know which activity types to use when?

You may have noticed that most chapters in this book have all three types of activities. The 'pre-test' sections at the start of each chapter have most of the comprehension and reflection activities, and the 'practical application' sections at the end of the chapters have most of the 'application to real life' activities.

The reason you'll always find these activities in the same places in each chapter is because various parts of your lesson structure lend themselves to different types of activities. You wouldn't put an application activity (getting learners to use their new skills in real-life scenarios) before you've demonstrated why, how and when to do it correctly, right?

Remember the best-practice structure from chapter 5? These types of activities lend themselves to the following parts:

- **The why – reflection and/or comprehension activities:** Show me what you already know. How does the 'why' motivate you to learn?
- **The theory and demonstration – comprehension activities:** Show me what you've learnt.
- **The practical – reflection and/or application activities:** Show me what and how you're going to do things differently.

Again, if you'd like a demonstration of this, have a look at the types of activities provided throughout this book. Each chapter follows a very similar pattern for a good reason. If you keep a similar pattern to your lessons, slides or chapters, your learners will appreciate the standardised approach to thinking, learning and doing – and be prepared for what's coming up next in each lesson.

What are my top recommendations for creating effective visual aids?
These are my top tips that apply to slides, workbooks or handouts.

Structure, structure, structure
This is so important an entire chapter is dedicated to it (chapter 5).

Minimalism is the way forward
Do you cram your slides and handouts full of information? If so, this is a sure-fire way to ensure your learners remember very little. Providing all the information on a slide or in a workbook makes the learning experience a more passive, forgettable experience. Use key words for bullet points, not whole sentences. Don't provide the entire picture immediately, and instead uncover it piece by piece and ask learners to predict what's coming next. Less is more. Less information from you means more thinking and interaction from your learners.

Questions are king
Have you noticed how many question marks I've included on each page in this book? Go have a quick count. Pick random pages. I'd be very surprised if you can find a page without one!

Human nature dictates that as soon as you're asked a question, you start wondering what the answer might be. This is the core of discovery-based learning – setting learners up to predict answers, and then finding out whether they're on the right track.

A quick word on animations
I have no objections to bullet points being animated in your presentation. However, make sure your animations:
- are timed to 'appear' as you start talking about that point
- only appear in the simplest way possible (not flying in, twirling, bouncing, or any of the other theatrical options PowerPoint offers)
- are dimmed when you've finished speaking about them.

So why animate bullet points? If you don't, all of the bullets come up at the same time and learners can't listen effectively if they're trying to read something else as well. Dimming the points after you've finished discussing them also helps your learners focus on the current point.

Tutorials on these aspects are available online, and links are included on the Resources page on my website.

> ## Demonstrate with clear examples
>
> In this section, my aim is to:
> - not recreate the wheel
> - send learners out to watch something that is already publicly available
> - create questions so they know whether they need to watch or not, and what they're listening out for
> - provide answers so they can test their knowledge.
>
> I'm going to demonstrate this idea so you can be a learner in the process and decide whether it's a strategy you'd like to employ in your own classroom. Play along, or skip ahead to the practical tasks.
>
> ## Would you like a quick lesson on how to use PowerPoint effectively?
>
> The online video 'How to avoid death by PowerPoint' (link provided on the Resources page on my website) outlines five clear principles – along with a whole heap of other great tips and tricks – to make your presentations as engaging as possible.
>
> The following questions help learners summarise the content in the video. If you're confident you know the answers, skip ahead to the practical tasks! If you're not sure you know the answers,

either watch the video to find out, or read the answers I've provided on the Resources page.

How do you ensure your PowerPoints are as engaging as possible?

Ask yourself:
- Do learners have a lot or a little working memory?
- How many 'messages' is recommended per slide?
- What happens if you try to listen to someone talking and read the information on the slides at the same time?
- If you have a lot of text on a slide, where should you cut and paste it into?
- What should you replace whole sentences with?
- What do humans tend to focus on?
- Which part of each slide should be the biggest?
- What can you use to keep learners focused on the message?
- What is the presentation, and what is the visual aid?
- What takes 500 per cent more time and energy than 'seeing'?
- How many objects should you have on a slide?
- Is having fewer slides better?

Practical application – your turn!

Practical task 8a: Visual aids planner

What type of visual aids do you use? How do you use them? Is it in ways that promote discovery-based learning? Consider the following options:
- slides
- workbooks
- technical posters or diagrams
- handouts or cheat sheets, manuals, textbooks, or reference material
- flashcards, whiteboard, sticky notes
- realia (real objects such as tools, equipment, machinery)
- videos.

Practical task 8b: Visual aids assessment criteria

Use the following criteria to assess your slide decks. How many can you check with confidence?

- **Style:**
    - Slides are visually engaging (not distracting), with standardised colours and fonts (that are on brand).
    - Images and content are balanced in the available space.
    - Layout, design, sizing and branding is streamlined.
    - Animations are appropriate and timely to encourage discovery learning, including dimming feature.
- **Content:**
    - All visual aids adhere to a structure of promising an outcome, showing the 'why', pre-testing, and providing the theory, a clear demonstration, an activity that will help learners achieve the promised outcome, and a recap to review main points.
    - Slides mostly contain key words only, and sentences only where absolutely necessary.
    - Appropriate amount of content used per slide (10 to 12 words max, including question or title).
    - Graphs, charts or images *demonstrate* your point.
    - Correct grammar and spelling used.
    - Questions (as slide titles) align to a workbook or achieving outcomes.
    - Consistent numbering system used on both the workbooks and the slides.
    - Comprehension, reflection and application activities included to achieve outcomes.
    - Adequate 'white space' provided for note taking (in workbooks).
    - Large 'chunks' of theory are absent from slides or workbooks (with links out to theory used).

Key takeaways
The core principles for creating effective visual aids are as follows:
- Visual aids should assist discovery-based learning by questioning, engaging and making learners think actively.
- Passive learning (spoonfeeding information) is less effective than active learning experiences.
- Well-designed visual aids put learners in the driver's seat, encouraging questioning and discovery-based learning.
- Visual aids are more than just slides. They include posters, diagrams, reference materials, flashcards, whiteboards, sticky notes, realia and videos.

The problem with 'boring' technical content is often not the content itself but how visual aids are designed and delivered. The overall goal is to create engaging, interactive learning experiences rather than passive information transfer.

> **Chapter 8 reflection**
> Check your answers to the initial pre-test (stage 3 diagnostic) – how much have you learnt? What are your biggest takeaways from this chapter? What will you do differently?

CHAPTER 9

Use techniques to build rapport and maximise engagement

The outcome

Use communication techniques to build rapport with your learners and maximise engagement

The why

Why is it important to build rapport with your learners?

If you don't, it's like talking to a room full of strangers who aren't connecting with you, are glued to their devices, or can't wait to get out of the classroom. How effective a learning experience do you think that can be?

Building rapport is also about creating a trusted learning environment – a place where learners can ask questions, check their understanding, and know they are in a 'safe', non-judgemental learning space where they're fully involved in the learning experience and not just a passive observer. All the visual aids and interactive activities in the world won't help you if your learners are too afraid to answer.

Creating this trusted learning environment is about not only verbal communication but also non-verbal communication techniques. No-one wants to turn up to a classroom to be taught by an uninspiring lecturer who appears rude or disrespectful. This, unfortunately, is what can happen when a mismatch exists between cultural expectations,

CHAPTER 9: Use techniques to build rapport and maximise engagement ■ 163

even if the facilitator is doing what they consider to be best practice in their own culture.

Having a good structure, great visual aids and compelling examples are the foundations of a quality learning experience, but the *way* you communicate non-verbally can make these aspects fall flat or come alive. The amount you know about the cultures of your learners can also widen the trust gap or close it entirely.

What kind of atmosphere do you want to create?

Pre-test – do you really need this chapter?

The skills check and knowledge check for this chapter are in the stage 3 diagnostic on the Resources page on my website.

The 'what, when and how' (the theory)

In the coming sections, we're going to discuss a range of verbal and non-verbal techniques for building rapport and maximising engagement, but let's start first with a technique that is neither verbal nor non-verbal, but instead focuses on the way you *visually* communicate concepts.

Comparison tables

Dense sections of theory can be presented a few different ways to your learners. Instead of explaining, though, I'd prefer to demonstrate. Let's look at two different ways of presenting the same information – in a table or in a list – using the core learning content definitions and examples for this chapter. First, here's the information in a list:

- **Concept checking questions (CCQs):**
  - Questions that ascertain whether a learner has really understood a concept: 'We've just learnt about how to make chocolate. Can you tell me the first step in making chocolate?'
- **Question tags:**
  - Adding a short question fragment at the end of a sentence to confirm understanding of the point with the listener or reader: 'You don't like chocolate, do you?'
- **Negative questions:**
  - Asking a question in the negative instead of the affirmative: 'Don't you like chocolate?'
- **First person plural and involvement expressions:**
  - Using language which includes everyone: 'We all love chocolate.' *or* 'Who here loves chocolate?'
- **Eliciting:**
  - Asking questions to find out learners' knowledge (as opposed to lecturing): 'Who here knows about how to make chocolate?'
- **Storytelling:**
  - Using real-life examples to drive home a point: 'Let me tell you about the time I missed step 1 in the chocolate-making process. Once you've heard this you'll never make the same mistake, trust me!'

Now let's look at the same information in a table. Which do you think is easier to digest as a learner (if you didn't have a facilitator to help you process it)? Which version would help you explain the concepts to another learner? Why do you think one version is easier to interpret than the other?

CHAPTER 9: Use techniques to build rapport and maximise engagement ■ 165

Core learning content definitions and examples for this chapter

Technique	Definitions	Examples
Concept checking questions (CCQs)	Questions that ascertain whether a learner has really understood a concept	'We've just learnt about how to make chocolate. Can you tell me the first step in making chocolate?'
Question tags	Adding a short question fragment at the end of a sentence to confirm understanding of the point with the listener or reader	'You don't like chocolate, do you?'
Negative questions	Asking a question in the negative instead of the affirmative	'Don't you like chocolate?'
First person plural and involvement expressions	Using language which includes everyone	'We all love chocolate.' or 'Who here loves chocolate?'
Eliciting	Asking questions to find out learners' knowledge (as opposed to lecturing)	'Who here knows about how to make chocolate?'
Storytelling	Using real-life examples to drive home a point.	'Let me tell you about the time I missed step 1 in the chocolate-making process. Once you've heard this you'll never make the same mistake, trust me!'

The table makes it much easier to 'read' the information, doesn't it? (There's another 'question tag', in case you need another example.) Tables make it easier to compare and contrast the various definitions, and also to compare all the examples and definitions in a single line of sight, instead of having to search through lines of text. Providing a table is one strategy to help you, the facilitator, point out the differences if learners are struggling, because you can directly point out the similarities and differences between the various items.

Tables like these can also be 'cut up' in various ways so learners can be actively engaged in piecing the content together; for example, each box on the preceding table could be individual flashcards the learners have to piece together until they get the table in the right order.

So now we've covered the basic definitions and examples, why and how do you use these techniques to their best advantage?

Demonstrate with clear examples

These points are best demonstrated at the same time as they're explained, so here are all these terms again, with their 'whys' and 'hows', and more worked examples.

Using concept checking questions

Concept checking questions (CCQs) are the key to a facilitator truly understanding whether their learners have understood the core concepts. You're not asking your learners to regurgitate what you just said; instead, you're focusing more about the second level thinking from Bloom's taxonomy (refer to chapter 4) where learners demonstrate *why* or *how* they understand. They help the facilitator ascertain the level of understanding of the core concepts among their learners.

So if I say something like, 'It's better to call someone and have a conversation rather than email them if it's a potentially touchy subject so you can make sure that the right tone and volume are used to reassure the other party'.

CCQs might be:
- 'If it's a potentially touchy subject, is it better to call or email? Why?'
- 'If you send an email, what might be misunderstood? Why?'

When a learner can explain back to you in their own words, there's a better chance they've understood the what, why and how of what you've just taught.

Other ways of asking CCQs is using phrases like:
- 'Can you explain that back to me in your own words?'
- 'What would you do in this situation? Can you explain why you'd do that?'
- 'If the reverse happened, what would you do? Why?'
- 'Tell me why this statement is true or false.'

Using CCQs puts the onus on your learners to engage with the lesson and check their understanding of the core concepts – taking the pressure off you to 'lecture', and also providing rock-solid evidence that your learners have taken on board what you were hoping to teach. It also shows you where the gaps in knowledge and understanding lie – so you can address them right there and then.

Using question tags

Question tags are designed to seek confirmation of an idea, and to invite conversation and discussion. They consist of a statement, and then a short question (which is negative if the statement is positive, and vice versa).

Examples include:
- This isn't correct, is it?
- This doesn't work, does it?
- We all do that, don't we?

The question can sometimes be rhetorical; you're not actually asking them to answer you out loud, but you are asking them to answer you in their heads.

Consider the difference between the following:
- 'Oh, we all do that.'
- 'We all do that, don't we?'

Do you see how the second option sounds so much softer, more friendly and inclusive, and also invites anyone who doesn't agree to discuss? The first option just states a fact, assuming it's true for all listeners and doesn't invite discussion.

Question tags can also have different inflections, which change the intention of the question. Try saying any of the three examples provided out loud – once with an upwards inflection at the end (which will sound more like a real question), and once with a downwards inflection (which will sound more like you're confirming your understanding).

Either way, using question tags is a way of making your statements a little more conducive to collaborative discussions rather than outright lecturing.

Using negative questions

Negative questions are another way to get your learners engaged in the discussion:

- 'Don't we all do that?'
- 'Isn't that right?'
- 'Don't you hate it when that happens?'

Much like using question tags, using negative questions is just a different way to invite discussion and connect with your audience.

Using first person plural and involvement expressions

First person plural and involvement expressions are similar in that, in both cases, you're including the other person.

When it's 'I', 'I', 'I' all the time, it's all about *you*, not your learners – this is another way facilitators can unknowingly disconnect from their learners.

Use 'we' and expressions that involve your learners, such as:

- 'What does everyone think?'
- 'Who agrees that this is a false statement?'
- 'How would we deal with this problem?'
- 'It would be really good if you and I could do this.'
- 'If you've got any problem with this course, then please get in touch with us and ask for help.'

CHAPTER 9: Use techniques to build rapport and maximise engagement ■ 169

By using these expressions, you're involving your learners in the conversation. You're not just prattling information from your podium, but actively including and involving your learners in the subtext of what you're saying. You'll find multiple examples of this throughout this book – that is, me involving you, the reader, in the conversation.

Using eliciting (as opposed to lecturing)

'Eliciting' is a fancy way of saying 'asking questions to get learners offering information that will guide the learning process rather than giving information by lecturing'.

You've read a lot about questions already in this book so I'm not going to hammer on about how awesome they are again, but I *am* going to give you a demonstration.

> **So how do you elicit responses? (Pause now and think about your answer to that question for five seconds before going on.)**

Well, I'm doing it right now – giving you the time to think and a chance to answer that question in your head first. The idea is that if you answer the question in your head first, whatever I say next you'll be thinking, *Oh, I was right!* or *Oh, I was completely wrong!*

Think about what you would instantly think if I said to you, 'How old do you think the Indigenous culture of Australia is?'

Human nature dictates that you'll immediately start sifting through your pre-existing knowledge to try to arrive at an answer. Then, as soon as the answer is revealed, you'll remember whether you were right or wrong.

(No, I'm not giving you the answer. If you want to know (or confirm) the answer to that question, you'll need to look it up. And, no, I'm not being lazy! #PractiseWhatIPreach #AntiSpoonFeedingTechnique.)

So have a quick think about how often *you* elicit when you have learners in front of you. How do you do it? What words do you use?

What happens if no-one answers? What happens if the room is filled with awkward silences? (See, I'm doing it now – getting you to answer these questions in your head first before I spill the beans.) These are all very good questions – and ones I will answer.

Here are some basic techniques for eliciting with success:
- You first ask a question.
- Then you leave a big long pause.
  - This can be quite frightening if no-one answers but hold your ground!
  - Sometimes no-one will answer even after a pause, but oftentimes people do (especially if you've built that strong, safe connection with them already).
- If no-one is answering, you can prompt them. Give them hints or some more context to jog their memory banks.
- If still no-one answers, try asking whether they think *xyz* is the right answer – or *abc*? Or *def*? Often presenting the right answer among some red herrings can encourage learners to have a go.
- If someone gives an incorrect answer, you can do a few different things:
  - Encourage them ('that's close!' or 'nice idea!') and then
    - ask the other learners if they have any other ideas
    - give them more context like, 'I was thinking more along the lines of *xyz*'.
  - Ask the other learners if they disagree or agree – often learners will have the same preconceived (incorrect) ideas so 'throwing it out there' to the rest of the learners really helps you as the facilitator to assess what foundational knowledge they have on the topic.
- If someone gives a correct answer, you can either:
  - Confirm they are correct and then
    - ask them to explain more (what you would have explained in your lecture)
    - carry on with more questions (or some demonstration).
  - Ask the other learners if they agree or disagree with that answer (another opportunity to check how many of your learners are across a certain topic or point).

CHAPTER 9: Use techniques to build rapport and maximise engagement ▪ 171

If you ask people what they think first, they're going to have a preconceived idea that you can then either quash or confirm. This is one of the basic principles of learning: to learn, you need to place new knowledge on top of what you already know. So, for this purpose:

- don't just give information – *elicit* responses
- ask for more responses
- ask learners to think about the answer to questions before you give them the answer
- give them time to think and to discuss with their peers (this is also a great hack for giving you a few extra moments to check your notes for what's coming up next).

Using storytelling

Storytelling is one of the best ways to build rapport. Of course, it brings a 'real', human element to what you're teaching, but it also helps learning. Remember the neuroscience from the previous chapter that explains the connection between humour, dopamine and retention of concepts in long-term memory? That's one of the reasons I've used real-life stories and examples with you in this book – like humour, stories can really stick with you, driving points home and helping you commit the learnings to long-term memory.

If you're going to tell stories, try to use 'direct speech' as much as possible – where you assume the characters of the story so your listeners feel like they're in the conversation with you. Have a read of this story about learning styles, for example.

> I remember when I had just got my driver's licence and, being from the country, I was new to driving in the city but had to learn quickly as I was moving there for university. I asked a guy at a service station (this was *long* before Google Maps existed) for directions to the closest supermarket. He said, 'Sure!' Then gave me a raft of instructions one after the other, like:
>
> > 'First you turn left at the roundabout, then you go straight, then after a couple of roundabouts turn right, and then after that there's a set of lights and a Bunnings on the corner …'

I said something like, 'You lost me at the first roundabout', to which he replied, 'Yeah, sorry, I probably went too fast', and then repeated all the instructions again, to which I responded by just standing there and looking dumb, and then saying, 'Thanks for that – super helpful!'

Now the reality was that I just walked back to my car and used the *UBD* (the old-fashioned paperback version of Google Maps we used in Western Australia) because that many audio instructions was just *too many* for me to process all at once. But see or draw a picture of exactly the same instructions? I'd barely need to look at it twice! That's how I learnt that I was much more visual dominant when it comes to processing directions!

Did this happen to you as a child? Were you made to believe that you were stupid or 'not quick enough' when the reality was you just weren't being taught in the right way?

How much more engaging is the story being told that way, rather than this way?

I asked a guy at a service station (this was *long* before Google Maps existed) for directions to the closest supermarket. He was very helpful but told me the directions one after the other until he had finished but there were too many for me to process that quickly. I told him I got confused, but he thought he went too fast so repeated the same instructions but slower. I listened, still confused, but because I was embarrassed, I just thanked him for being helpful and left. I didn't realise at the time that I wasn't a strong audio learner but learnt later in life that seeing maps was much easier for me to understand and remember.

The 'what, when and how' (the theory) *continued* ...

How do you build confidence with delivering your content?

The following three confidence-building techniques aren't particularly groundbreaking. If you're using the questioning and discussion-provoking techniques explained already in this chapter, it really does just come down to practice, practice, practice.

Remember – it's never about reaching 'perfection', because that's not what lifelong learning is all about. Good teaching experiences will morph over time as you grow as a facilitator, and as cohorts of learners come and go.

You'll always gain more experience and more examples with every class you teach. Embrace the learning curve by:

- **Speaking from the heart instead of from your notes.** Practise in front of an empty classroom if that helps you get more fluency and flow to what you're saying.
- **Using real-life examples and demonstrations from your experience.** You're in the facilitator chair because you've been there, done that, and can pass on your experience. Learners can find the theory on Google, AI or YouTube. Use your personal experience and life lessons in your classes and watch your learners 'switch on'.
- **Acknowledging questions, even when you're not sure of the answer.** Getting an answer that is clearly not confident or is actually wrong from someone who is meant to be an expert on the topic is pretty frustrating. Having said that, experts are not encyclopaedias either; you're only human! Have the courage to say, 'Ooooer, great question. I'm not sure about the answer to that one but I'll have a look and get back to you!', or throw the question back to the other learners and say, 'Ooooer, great question. What does everyone else think the answer to that question is?' That approach will buy you a little more time to process your response, and if you're not 100 per cent sure you know the right answer, promise to have the answer for the next class. There's no shame in admitting that you don't have encyclopaedic knowledge; in fact, as a learner, I'd prefer to know you can admit when you're not sure rather than feeding us something that's partially true or entirely incorrect – wouldn't you?

How about non-verbal communication techniques?

These techniques are much easier to identify and not really rocket science. So instead of me boring you by explaining them, you decide – which of the following items do you think are recommended, and which aren't?

- **Posture:**
  - shoulders down, slumped, back to the audience
  - shoulders back, standing up straight, chest open to the audience.
- **Gestures:**
  - hands in pockets, arms hanging, arms crossed over chest, fidgeting
  - using hands to emphasis/reinforce your points, using thumbs up/down.
- **Eye contact:**
  - looking down, at the wall, at the ceiling or only at half of the learners
  - looking at all learners, scanning the whole room, using 'anchors' (definition provided after list).
- **Using the space:**
  - standing in one spot, or pacing the length of the room
  - moving around to address all learners, moving 'to their level'.
- **While learners are working independently:**
  - taking a break and checking your phone for message or updates
  - walking around the room listening and monitoring learner progress through tasks.

'Anchors' refer to people at various extremities in the room – far left, far right, back, front and in the middle. If you have trouble making eye contact with your learners, find someone at each extremity (or at least in different areas of the room) who is looking at you and has a friendly face, and rotate maintaining eye contact with all of them. That way, your eyes will be making contact with learners all over the room, which is better than just focusing on one side of the room or on no-one at all!

If you didn't choose the second option in each of the preceding examples, you may be from a completely different culture to me! Although those options might look obvious to you if you've been raised

CHAPTER 9: Use techniques to build rapport and maximise engagement ■ 175

in bog-standard suburban Australian culture, they might not be for people who have been raised in different backgrounds.

Is non-verbal communication the same in all cultures?
The simple answer here is *no*. Although all of the four items in the following list show assertiveness, honesty and politeness in the culture I was raised in, do you know what they can mean in different cultures?
- Holding eye contact.
- Placing hands on your hips.
- Making the AOK sign with your hand.
- Shaking hands with someone when you meet them.

In different cultures I've lived in, I've found out the hard way that these things can indicate both aggressiveness and arrogance. The AOK sign, for example, is an absolute minefield. Did you know it can mean 'money', 'okay', 'worthless' or an indication of sexual orientation, depending on the country you're in? And if you hold up your little finger only, it could mean anything from 'you can't fool me', to 'that's bad', 'female', 'skinny' or 'reduced masculinity', depending on whether you're in Europe, Asia or South America? Yikes! Almost makes you want to keep your hands in your pockets at all times, doesn't it?

Here are some other cultural life lessons I've learnt the hard way:
- In Indonesia, standing with your hands on your hips is considered a sign of arrogance. And, yes, even though I have known this for nearly 30 years, because it's such a natural way to wait around in my own culture, I still find myself waiting in Indonesia with my hands on my hips, before I catch myself and hurriedly drop my arms.
- In Asia I've beckoned people to come closer by using a gesture that is usually reserved for animals – palm up instead of palm down, which is the gesture reserved for humans in those cultures.
- I've greeted an African student with a firm handshake and been met with a very limp one, which impressed neither of us until we started talking about handshakes in different cultures and what they mean. (Firm handshakes indicate aggression in his culture; limp handshakes indicate weakness of character in mine.)

- When I first started teaching nearly 30 years ago, I tried to get a young unmarried Muslim woman to work with an unmarried man in a paired activity. Her response was to flee from the room in tears. Clueless, another student had to point out to me how incredibly inappropriate that request had been. Mortifying.
- I've been sneered at for trying to maintain eye contact with a class full of male students in the Middle East, and then laughed at in the staff room when I dared to wonder out loud about the sexual orientation of most of them. (It's completely normal for men to hold hands and greet each other with kisses in this culture, although they would never do those things with women they're not married to – basically the opposite of how I was raised.)
- I've patted a kid on the head in Thailand and also rested my feet on a stool so the soles of my feet pointed directly at the restaurant owner, completely ignorant of the fact that both of these actions are highly disrespectful in Thai culture.
- I was reprimanded by my students at an end-of-year celebration in Japan for pouring myself a drink at the table and resting my chopsticks in my bowl. The first action indicated that I thought everyone at the table was rude for not pouring me a drink already, and the second action was rude because the only place you leave chopsticks *in* a bowl is when you're leaving them there for the next person to retrieve the remaining bones from a cremation casket.
- Remember the story from chapter 1 about the Afghani interpreters who were so horrified that we suggested men could also do domestic chores such as cleaning toilets and doing the laundry that they left the classroom in disgust?

Oh, the ways I have failed, and learnt by humiliation. All I can say from my experience is that if you're working with people from different cultures, you're best off doing some research into what is and isn't considered rude in their culture. This allows you to at least be aware of and make allowances for both your own behaviour and theirs.

This was reinforced for me just recently. Remember that group of lecturers, also from chapter 1, who I was training from the vocational college and were getting unsavoury reviews from their international

CHAPTER 9: Use techniques to build rapport and maximise engagement ■ 177

students? I asked them what behaviours they considered rude from their international students and 'sniffing' (instead of blowing your nose) was right up there. They were horrified to learn that blowing your nose in public and then folding the tissue and putting it in your pocket was as disgusting in some Asian cultures as it would be for us to poop in public, and then carry the poopy toilet paper around in our pockets. You can only imagine how disgusted and humiliated an Asian student might have been to be told to blow their nose in front of the rest of the class; once the lecturers understood this, all of a sudden the unsavoury reviews started making sense.

So how *do* you deal with situations like this where you have a clash in what is considered rude or unsavoury behaviour in different cultures?

In my experience, it's all about initiating hard discussions. Although they might be difficult or awkward at the time, they will ultimately help you to create a safe, trusted learning environment. Bringing these conversations out into the open is usually far more productive than silently wishing the issues would go away. Once people open up to the differences, they can learn to respect each other and find a compromise. Once the trainers in that session at the vocational college understood that there was actually a major difference in how they and their students dealt with a runny nose, for example, they agreed that discussing this in class, and getting all the students to understand what was considered rude and not rude in their various cultures, would create a more tolerant and understanding learning space, and actually bring the teachers and students closer.

My other piece of advice when working with people from other cultures is to remember that you simply don't know what you don't know. If something seems 'off' to you, be curious. Ask questions. Do some googling. You might be surprised by what you find out.

We didn't follow this approach when I was working in the Pacific, until it was way too late.

We'd been working with the lecturers at the vocational college for over a year by the time I was delivering a leadership training session for them. The session involved categorising behaviours as 'assertive', 'aggressive' and 'passive'. We discussed the definitions of each of those words, and then started working through the examples. Everything seemed to be going fine, until I asked: 'Okay, next one – telling your boss exactly what you want. Passive, aggressive or assertive?' The entire room of 25 lecturers yelled out, 'AGGRESSIVE'. Thinking I hadn't read out the example properly, or perhaps had been misunderstood, I asked the question again – and received the same answer.

It was quite surreal. I checked again, saying, 'Not yelling or shouting, just telling your boss what you want if they ask you directly what you want'. Again, they all agreed this was aggressive behaviour. I was speechless as the pennies started to drop, and they could tell. One very brave lecturer stood up and said, 'Maria, in your culture it's good to tell your boss what you want? Do you really want our opinions?'

I could have cried. In fact, just writing about this now brings tears to my eyes. It had felt, at times, like we'd been metaphorically beating our heads against a brick wall. At meeting after meeting, we'd asked the lecturers for input or at least to tell us what they thought about the plans we had for implementing the next stages of the project. We'd be met with silence, silence and more silence. Exasperated, we'd come to the conclusion that they either didn't care or had no opinions. So we blindly kept plodding in a direction we thought they'd be supportive of, with very little indication (according to our culture) that this was true.

That brave lecturer then explained that silence was the way agreement was conveyed in the *maneaba* (the local community meeting place where all important things happened). Speaking up and giving an opinion was reserved for the respected elders in the community, to whom the community turned for guidance when things needed to happen. So by giving us their silence, they had been respectfully giving us their agreement the whole time, which we had erroneously thought was indifference, disagreement or having no opinion.

Can you imagine how much more productive that first year of the project would have been if we had known this incredibly important element of Kiribati culture?

You simply don't know what you don't know – and when you're working with people from different cultures it really is on *you* to do your research if your aim is to create a trusted, safe learning environment. Do the research. Be curious. Have the hard conversations. You might surprise yourself!

Practical application – your turn!
Practical task 9: Rapport-building techniques
How many of these techniques do you use in your everyday teaching? Which ones could you be open to using more of? Consider the following techniques:
- comparison tables (as opposed to lists)
- concept checking questions (CCQs)
- question tags
- negative questions
- first person plural and involvement expressions
- eliciting (as opposed to lecturing)
- storytelling
- using all of the available space in the classroom
- monitoring while learners work independently
- being curious about learners' cultures.

If you'd really like to challenge yourself, record a session that you deliver to a group of learners and review the recording by listening out for how many times you use these techniques. Critique the delivery and consider at what stages you could have used these techniques more.

If you don't have a recording of yourself presenting, try reviewing a lesson that you've signed up for as a learner. Did the presenter use these techniques? Did it help build rapport with you as a learner?

Key takeaways
The key takeaways about techniques to build rapport with learners and maximise engagement are as follows:
- Building rapport creates a trusted learning environment where learners feel safe to ask questions and fully engage rather than being passive observers.
- Confidence with content is essential for building trust with learners. This means being able to speak from the heart, provide clear examples and answer questions about basic principles without heavily relying on notes.

- Non-verbal communication varies significantly across cultures; gestures, body language, and behaviours that are perfectly acceptable in one culture can be considered rude, offensive or inappropriate in others.
- Common cross-cultural misunderstandings can significantly impact the effectiveness of your learning environment.
- Cross-cultural communication requires awareness and research – proactively learning about cultural norms helps prevent misunderstandings and embarrassment, and having honest, sometimes uncomfortable, conversations about cultural expectations creates mutual understanding.
- Curiosity and openness are essential attributes – approaching cultural differences with genuine interest rather than judgement creates better outcomes.

> **Chapter 9 reflection**
>
> Check your answers to the initial pre-test (stage 3 diagnostic) – how much have you learnt? What are your biggest takeaways from this chapter? What will you do differently?

Where to now?

Now we have connected with our learners, structured a comprehensive curriculum, and learnt how to design and deliver learning resources that keep our learners engaged and motivated. What else can there be? Continuous improvement. You can always learn and improve, and this next stage takes you through all the ways you can do this when you're a teacher.

OUTCOME: Use feedback from your learners to improve your professional practice

STAGE 4

CRITIQUE: Continuous improvement

Regardless of how well you've met learner needs, structured your lessons or delivered your learning materials, there's always room for improvement or things to learn from how and why things went well (or not so well). This is why the keyword for this stage is *critique* – you need to do this with every aspect of the teaching and learning process. This stage is about being committed to continuously improving, making the best out of any situation, and growing and learning from every experience.

You need to not only ask for feedback, but also know how to process all types of feedback. And this includes the last thing most people want to deal with – the 'ugly' feedback, if and when it comes in! We've all been taught by people who are clearly recycling the same content over and over again, and also by those who have clearly never taken on any feedback and are set in their (not particularly effective) ways. I'm sure you've also known what it's like to be in front of a professional who not only asks for feedback but also is genuinely interested and concerned about making your experience as effective as it can be, taking on board advice and changing the way they do things as a result.

Which type of professional do you want to be seen as?

If you really want to commit to continuous improvement, you'll need to use feedback from your learners to reflect on and improve your professional practice. This process has several stages:
- provide, request and receive feedback
- process feedback
- implement a reflective practice.

These are the focus for the last three chapters of this book. If you're pretty sure you've got this stage covered already, confirm it by doing the stage 4 diagnostic on the Resources page on my website. (Scan the QR code to access.)

Please note this chapter does not cover organisational training needs analysis (because that's a whole other book), and is instead aimed more at the course or presentation level.

I've included some ripper tear-jerker stories in this chapter – so even if you do 'score' highly on the diagnostic, I'd still recommend skimming through the chapters, even if it's just for the stories!

CHAPTER 10

Provide, request and receive feedback

The outcome

Provide, request and receive feedback

The why

Is continuous improvement really the key to rave reviews?

Yes, yes it is. It doesn't matter whether we're talking about giving feedback to your learners, or them giving feedback to you. Living by the principle of lifelong learning, or continuous improvement, is the key to your learners achieving their goals faster and your training getting better every time you deliver it.

No-one wants to be *that* facilitator – the one who is stuck in their ways, recycles the same content over and over, and bores the socks off every group of people who comes before them to learn. We've all been there, in that classroom, thinking, *Gee I'd love to give this guy some feedback but I'm assuming it will just fall on deaf ears so there's probably no point*' … right?

You don't want to be that trainer, do you? The following are actual reviews given to trainers at a government organisation in Australia. Which of these reviews would you prefer to receive?

- 'Training material appeared to be very old and would benefit from being reviewed on an annual basis.'
- 'Great relevance to my job, well-presented and presenter has good relevant experience in the subject. You can tell he's up to date with what happens on the job.'

- 'The practice activities weren't supervised and a high number failed due to incorrect practice but didn't realise.'
- 'I really struggled to see the PowerPoint and whiteboard from where I was sitting at the back of the room.' (Feedback given at the end of an 11-week course.)

I'm assuming you'd prefer the second one, and would be mortified to receive any of the others.

Is providing, requesting and receiving feedback really necessary?

No, not if you have no desire to improve. (Oof, that's a lot of double negatives there. The point is that, yes, feedback is absolutely necessary if you want to improve.)

Feedback is also necessary (and can be legally mandatory) if you are employed as a trainer in a formalised qualifications framework – for example, the Australian Qualifications Framework (AQF). Delivering training to AQF standards means that you *will* need to give feedback and collect both evidence and feedback as part of your job role.

What does your job, workplace or training system require?

Check whether the following apply:
- Is collecting and providing feedback mandatory or a 'nice to have'?
- Do you know whether you need to collect competency-based evidence? Are personal comments required? Is there a grading system? Should you be giving detailed written or just verbal feedback with improvement suggestions?
- Is the type of feedback you give and record detailed enough so that if you're audited you can remember specific details about the person you've collected evidence about?

If the answer to any of those questions is 'no', 'not really', or 'I'm not sure', it's a good idea to find out now, so you can decide which parts of this chapter will be most useful for you. Please also note that this chapter offers general recommendations that need to be adapted based on the needs and protocols within your organisation.

Pre-test – do you really need this chapter?

The skills check and knowledge check for this chapter are in the stage 4 diagnostic on the Resources page on my website.

The 'what, when and how' (the theory)

Do you know what is legally or contractually required of you as a trainer?

If you're not legally or contractually required to give and receive feedback, this next section won't really apply to you so skim through or skip ahead to the section after the next lightbulb.

If you are legally or contractually required to give and receive feedback or evidence, it's a good idea to verify with your employer as soon as possible how, where and when you will assess and record the competencies and/or evidence required to prove achievement of the outcomes. It's also wise to ask if any marking guides or instructions exist on what is required to pass or fail tasks, and the process by which you need to record, store and submit it.

Why is it important to collect evidence in a thorough, systematic way?

If you're required by law to collect evidence, you need to make sure it will stand up when it's crunch time. (Auditing – always a joy!)

If I asked you about a learner you had a year ago, consider:

- Could you remember the reasons you assessed them as competent or not yet competent?
- Would the evidence you collected give you enough information to specifically recall that learner above all the other learners you've had?

If an accident in the workplace was caused by a learner you had deemed 'competent' in the skill that caused the accident, would you have sufficient proof and be able to defend your position?

No? Not good. Let's make sure that doesn't happen, shall we?

How do you collect feedback that is memorable enough to satisfy the toughest auditing process?

I've got a few strategies you can employ to take the stress out of wondering whether or not you've compiled enough memorable evidence.

Create a learner file

Whatever way is easiest for you (pen and paper, on 'Notes' on your phone, on a document you keep on your computer), create a learner file for each learner you're working with. Record aspects that will help you remember them as a person – their personality, the way they work with others, anything that will help you build a picture to remember them 12 months down the track.

Keep records of times they attempted tasks but didn't quite reach 'competence' and why

Remembering the journey a learner has gone through to become competent is just as important as them being labelled as competent at a certain point in time.

Being able to remember the mistakes they made or any attempts that were almost on the mark will again help you recreate the story of that learner and how they progressed under your supervision. If you're collecting feedback from your learners, include this in their file too, because this may also provide extra information about what they struggled with or what extra help they asked for.

When they are deemed competent, record as much detail as possible

When? Where? With whom? In what scenarios? What was the task they were working on and what process did they go through to achieve competence? Record as many details as you can so that in the event you need to remember why the learner was deemed competent, you have more than enough to recreate the scene. Include dates, times, places and as much other information as necessary.

> 💡 It's your responsibility to pass a learner as 'competent' but simply 'knowing' that they are isn't enough. Think about *why* they are and *how* they got there. This is what you need to be able to remember, possibly many months and many other learners after you've signed them off.

Why is it important to use feedback strategies that include self-assessment, peer assessment and concept checking?

Have you ever heard the expression, 'many hands make light work'? In a nutshell, that's what using a range of feedback strategies does.

It takes the pressure off *you* (the facilitator) to do all the work, and spreads the load between your learners, their peers and yourself.

Ask yourself the following questions:

- Do you employ a 'self-assessment first' strategy with your learners? (In other words, do they critique themselves first before you give them feedback?)
- Do you employ a 'peer assessment' strategy where appropriate? (This means they critique each other before you give them feedback.)
- Once you give them feedback, do you ask your learners to summarise and paraphrase your suggestions/recommendations/assessment comments to show they've understood your feedback and how they can improve?

If you answered no to any of these questions, you're just making more work for yourself, and creating learners who depend on you for all aspects of assessment or practical skills feedback – which can be very draining!

Learning how to encourage self- and peer-review as a standard practice in your learning environments will make your work load easier.

Why can peer assessment be so powerful?

Peer assessment is getting your learners into pairs or small groups and asking them to observe their peers doing a task so they can decide whether they are achieving the outcomes or assessment criteria satisfactorily.

Why does this work? If learners can see someone else perform the task to standard (or not), they have a better chance of self-correcting when they're doing the task themselves.

Ever been in a position where you're watching someone else do something and you can easily point out whether they're 'doing it right'? When you put someone through a microscope, you're way more likely to be more critical of the way you do things yourself, which is the premise of peer assessment and why it works so well.

How do you create peer assessment opportunities?

It really depends on the task, and the complexity of the outcomes or assessment criteria.

Where possible, break the task down into its smallest parts, and get your learners taking turns to do parts of the task so they can assess each other as they go. Small groups work best – in a group of three, one can do the task while the other two observe. After feedback, group members can rotate so everyone gets a turn observing and being observed. Hopefully, their skills can build as they watch and learn from their peers attempting the same tasks.

If you can do this as an in-class activity, when learners run into problems or if they disagree on certain criteria, they can ask for your guidance. This also highlights anything that a large percentage of your learners are struggling with, which might indicate that you need to provide more explicit teaching or demonstration on that point.

Is this something you could implement in your classroom? If you do, make sure you have a list of marking criteria or points that learners can 'critique' their peers on (rather than asking for a global 'yeah, they can do it okay' level of feedback). Without marking criteria, such activities can have the opposite effect from that desired, and actually be quite destructive. Here's a cautionary tale for you!

I was talking to a very dedicated student currently studying engineering in Norway, and he was voicing his frustrations with peer assessment. As an avid supporter of the technique, I was curious as to why he wasn't enjoying it. The student explained the lecturer had not given them any criteria to assess by, so the students were literally making up their feedback out of thin air. So, in this young man's words, 'It's *stupid*. A complete waste of time. I have no idea if I am wrong or his assessment of me is wrong. I don't think he knows what he's talking about but the teacher won't help. I'm even more confused now'. Peer assessment can be a powerful tool – when set up correctly!

What is self-assessment and why do it?

Good question. Have you been in a situation where an assessor, an examiner or a manager has asked you how you think you've gone (with a task, assessment or performance) and you immediately think of all the things you could have done better? You're not alone – it's a very common response.

Self-assessment is key to learning, and it's why I start every chapter with a pre-test section. If you're willing to self-assess and admit where you may not have the skills and knowledge, you're more open to receiving constructive feedback and absorbing new knowledge.

How do you create self-assessment opportunities?

Test-teach-test

I've hammered on about this strategy throughout this book, so I'm not going to repeat myself here. #TestTeachTest4Life

Pre-final assessment self-reflection activities

Ask learners to assess themselves against the criteria, stating why or why not they should be deemed competent. It can be quite eye-opening to see how much false confidence a learner has, or how over-critical they are of their performance. Either way, it's a good indicator for you to know how to create assessment opportunities that show both their strengths and the gaps in their skills and knowledge.

Being critical of yourself against the assessment criteria is a clear indication of how deeply you've taken on the knowledge and developed the necessary skill set. How often do you get your learners to put themselves under the microscope? Could you do it more often?

Facilitating self- and peer-assessment opportunities gives you a very clear insight into what assessment criteria your learners have a handle on, and which ones they need more instruction, demonstration or practice on before being formally assessed or deemed competent.

It also shines a very clear light on what *you* need to focus on when teaching the next round of learners. Every group of learners will present with different issues and roadblocks. The more you're aware, the better you can cater for the next round of learners.

Can you use concept checking questions when assessing a learner?

Of course! If you can use concept checking questions (CCQ) to ascertain whether a learner fully understands a concept you've just taught, why wouldn't you use them to check their full understanding of how to achieve the outcomes or assessments you've provided?

Why is it important to ask for and receive useful feedback from your learners?

In a nutshell, you have no idea what's going on in your learners' heads unless you ask them. Regardless of whether or not you're giving *them* feedback as part of their assessment processes, it's vital that they also give *you* feedback on the job that you're doing as a trainer or facilitator.

If you're a lifelong learner, and believe you always have room for improvement, you'll know that asking for feedback is essential if you're going to improve the way you train and assess. Doing so also creates trust and a more open and friendly learning environment. What have you got to lose?

There is a catch, though: if you don't ask, you likely won't be told, unless you have built a good enough rapport with your learners that they're confident to approach you when something isn't right (or when something is really good).

If they're not confident enough to approach you, they'll either not say anything, or (if they're really unhappy) they'll go over your head to your superiors. Wouldn't you prefer to hear it directly from them? Whether it's good or bad?

Coming up in the next chapter, I share a whole bunch of feedback I've been given in the past, and how it ended up changing the way I taught forever.

When and how should you ask for feedback?

It depends on how long your course runs for, but the general rule is that you should ask for feedback not too long after you've started with your learners, somewhere around the middle and at the end. Here's what to keep in mind at each point:

- **Before or near the start:** Ask for feedback to ensure no barriers to learning exist that would make it difficult for the learners to take full advantage of the learning experience. Also, as the first section of this book outlined, getting to know your learners before you start working with them is important.
- **Midway:** Get feedback at this point to make sure nothing else has cropped up along the way. Sometimes you're unaware of how the smallest things can become serious barriers to learning, and a quick, simple fix could completely change the learning experience for your learners. However, if you don't know, you can't fix it! Wouldn't you be upset knowing that if you'd just asked, you could have removed a barrier to learning really easily, but instead your learners have been silently and unnecessarily suffering?
- **At the end:** Ask for feedback so you can get their opinion of the full learning experience. If you're also assessing learners, having separate questions for the 'learning' and the 'assessment' is wise because some learners may struggle with different parts of the full experience. For example, learners may rate a course quite highly until they receive their assessments back. If they're not happy with their results, their opinion of the learning experience (and the preparation you provided them for their assessments) may change dramatically.

Remember that master's unit from chapter 2 where we listened to 12 lectures (which were all quite interesting on some level, delivered by a very knowledgeable and experienced international relations professor), and I was awarded a C grade for my essay and then a D grade after appealing the grading process? Imagine the difference in my review of that class if I'd submitted it before I was graded, and afterwards. Definitely something to think about when timing your surveys!

Hang on, back up a bit – did I just recommend that you get feedback from your learners three times? *Three*? Isn't that going a bit OTT?

No. In fact, this is the *minimum* I'd recommend. It's even better if you can establish an ongoing way for your learners to give you feedback – at the end of every week (for longer courses) or every day (if it's a short course). Ask for feedback as much as possible because, like I said before, unless you've built rapport with your learners (or they're incredibly brazen, or they're millennials 😉), they're unlikely to approach you first.

Why do learners hold back feedback?

You might think, *But surely they'd tell me if they had a problem*? Not all the time. Learners often hold back feedback because they:

- think they're the only ones experiencing that issue
- think they must be a bit dumb, or have too high expectations on how much they're meant to grasp
- think you're incapable of processing the feedback, so don't even bother
- just have blind faith that because you're the facilitator/guru/master, you must know what's going on – which is definitely possible if you're a mind reader.

And that's just it. You're not a mind reader. Just because you're an expert in your field doesn't mean you can see what your learners can. In fact, often you are literally incapable of seeing it from their eyes because you haven't been at the same level of expertise as your learners for decades.

What you might think is 'common sense' or blindingly obvious, you may gloss over very quickly or barely cover in any detail because you don't want to bore your learners.

Take the first golf lesson I had just recently (because I love learning new things! #LifelongLearner). My teacher had been on the international circuit and had been playing golf for decades. This guy had pro-level expertise. Who wouldn't want to learn from the best? I was excited. But the lesson began like this. 'Right, so, the clubs – the bigger they are the further they go and the more angled they are the higher the ball will go into the sky before returning. Got it? Good. Let's move on to grip.'

No, I hadn't 'got it'. (I failed physics at school because I just couldn't grasp the concepts unless I was involved in the demonstration.) But I didn't have a chance to ask a question or repeat back what I had learnt so it literally went in one ear and out the other. (I just had to google golf club physics to write this story because I could not remember the connection between size and distance, or angle and height.)

Now imagine if instead he'd asked me a CCQ – like, 'Okay, so if you want it to not go very far, do you use a bigger club or a smaller one?' or, 'If you want it to go long and not so high, which size and which angle should you use?' Then he would have realised that I had completely missed this fundamental part of golfing physics. But he didn't, so he didn't.

Learning experiences are changeable from learner to learner. Throw in a good mix of cultures, ages and backgrounds and you can't possibly predict every issue or problem that a learner may find with your content, the way you're delivering or even things like technical issues. Regardless of how savvy your learners appear, you really have *no idea* what's going on beneath the surface – unless you *ask*.

If one person has a problem, they're likely not the only one but rarely do they realise that. Make a point of creating a learning environment that welcomes feedback and encourages questions. As a learner, if you know your facilitator is open to constructive criticism, you're going to be way more likely to give it and way less likely to hold back whatever it is that's troubling you.

Millennials (in Australian culture, at least) will be more likely to 'say it like it is' because this generation were encouraged to talk about their feelings. I'm generation X, and when I was at school, we wouldn't have *dreamed* of telling our teachers what we really thought of them for fear of being publicly shamed, ridiculed or punished. (I was once put on detention for asking a very sensible question about what would happen if I changed religions and then died: would I go to Catholic hell but Muslim heaven if I married a Muslim and started observing the Islamic faith? It was a fair question for a young teenager trying to get their head around world religions, but considering the punishment I received, I never asked that teacher an honest question again.) If you're working with gen X or older, they likely grew up in similar educational environments and will likely feel the same (unless they've been working in more progressive environments).

Make yourself approachable. Encourage questions. Use them to your advantage and as a learning experience for the whole class. I don't know about you but I'd be much happier with all that out in the open rather than festering away between learners after class! Wouldn't you?

Demonstrate with clear examples

How do you get effective feedback?

You ask for it. And you make it easy for your learners to respond. You can:

- do it as an in-class activity
- assign it as homework
- make it anonymous
- create complex questions
- keep it simple.

Pre-course survey example

As I mention in chapter 1, I've included a link to a survey I send to prospective clients on the Resources page on my website (under the resources for chapter 1 and this chapter). Keep in mind that the questions you'll need to ask your learners will depend on the type of course you're running, who your intended audience is likely to be and what outcomes they are hoping to achieve by working with you.

Remember that pre-course/presentation surveys can also include a list of knowledge-based questions (like I have provided in the diagnostics), which can help you ascertain the current knowledge and skill levels in your learners before they embark on a learning experience with you.

Mid- or end-of-course survey examples

Each of the following options have pros and cons, and are used for different reasons. Can you predict what they are and how you'd implement them?

In-class

This is a great way to get simple, on-time feedback that can guide the way you're delivering your class. Use digital survey software such as Google Forms or SurveyMonkey if you want detailed answers, or simple tools such as Mentimeter to gauge what people are thinking or feeling.

Apps like these are simple to use, easy to keep anonymous (or not) and can provide instant answers you can share with the class as soon as they come in. You can ask questions like:

- Who needs more practice at *[insert skill]*?
- Who needs more demonstrations or explanations of *[insert core concept]*?
- What's the hardest thing about *[insert concept, skill, or any teaching point]*?

This helps learners instantly see how the whole group feels – which can be helpful for them as well as you. They're also more likely to tell the truth (especially if you keep it anonymous) than if you were to ask the question in the old-fashioned 'hands up if you ...' way.

Another old-school way to do this is to get them to write their answers on a piece of paper, fold it and put it in a feedback box. You can then draw them out one by one, and summarise the results (obviously much slower than a digital version but quick and easy to do on the spot as needed).

Homework
This option is better for longer, more complex feedback, where you really want the learners to provide detailed explanations or examples. Again, you can use digital survey software, or create a document you want them to fill out and return digitally or on paper.

Anonymous
When feedback is anonymous, learners may be more likely to tell the truth, the whole truth and nothing but the truth. Especially for learners who don't have a lot of trust, or are quite new to the organisation or working with you, this option does remove some barriers to fully expressing what they really think or feel.

Complex
You can get an in-depth analysis of the course content, delivery style and technical concerns in an online survey or face-to-face chat. Every course is different so you'll need to focus on the core elements of your course and go from there – what feedback would you like regarding the content, tasks, delivery mode, facilitator performance, platform or venue?

Here are some simple questions to start with that would apply to most courses:
- How are you finding the course so far?
- Are you struggling with anything or need help with a particular area?
- Do you think anything is missing or not comprehensive enough?
- Could we do anything to make completing tasks easier for you?
- How are you finding the tasks? Are they too difficult to complete alone? Why/why not? Is it a lack of skill, content or experience, or are the instructions simply not clear enough?

You'll notice these are open-ended questions, meaning that learners can write free-flowing answers. You can also ask multiple choice questions, or ask learners to rate items on a scale of one to ten, or 'strongly agree' to 'strongly disagree'.

As with all course evaluation questions, the questions could be interpreted differently from what you intended, or the answers might not give you the insight you were looking for. Be careful in the types of questions you ask, and try to ensure only one way to answer the question is possible so it will give you a 'valid' response.

Looking for an easy way to start? Using a survey tool such as SurveyMonkey, you can use pre-validated questions, which have been created to avoid issues with misinterpretation by survey takers. If you don't have explicit experience in creating evaluation questions, this is a very good place to start to ensure the data you get back from your learners is of the highest quality.

I've also created a list of sample statements you can include in your surveys (regarding the delivery and content, learning and assessment materials, facilitators and venue or learning space), with a scale so learners can 'rate' from one to ten (one = strongly disagree, ten = strongly agree), or a six-point scale (including strongly disagree, disagree, unsure, agree, strongly agree or not applicable). (Access these questions via the Resources page on my website.)

I recommended leaving an open-answer question after each of the categories I provided in case learners would like to provide more information about any of the ratings they have given.

Simple

Sometimes simple is best! This is especially the case if you're doing more frequent, weekly surveys just to keep tabs on how your learners are progressing.

One of the quickest and most efficient surveys to use is called 'start, stop, continue'. It asks three simple questions:

- **Start:** What should we *start* doing that we're not already doing?
- **Stop:** What should we *stop* doing? What is unnecessary, a waste of time, confusing or just plain boring?
- **Continue:** What do you *love* about this course that you think we should definitely *continue* doing?

The same goes for using in-class activities to gauge how people are feeling or whether they've understood core concepts – ask CCQs on a Mentimeter and see what percentage of the class has gotten the core concepts, or test knowledge with quick impromptu quizzes.

Getting feedback from your learners doesn't have to be complex or time-consuming to prepare. It can be as simple as handing out pieces of paper and collecting answers to a pop quiz. Don't make it any more complex than it needs to be.

Practical application – your turn!

Practical task 10: Create your feedback strategy

Unsurprisingly, the task here is to create your own feedback strategy – including how you're going to give and receive feedback from your learners. Consider:

- How and when are you going to give your learners feedback about their progress, assessments or the achievement of the outcomes you've promised them?
- How are you going to implement feedback strategies such as peer review, self-assessment and CCQs?
- What are you going to include in and how are you going to deliver your:
  - pre-course survey
  - mid-course survey
  - end-of-course survey?

Key takeaways
Here are the key aspects to remember from this chapter:
- Legal and contractual requirements:
  - Trainers should verify assessment requirements with employers, including how to record, store and submit evidence.
  - Understanding legal requirements for evidence collection is crucial for audit purposes.
- Evidence collection best practice:
  - Create detailed learner files, recording specific information that can protect you if competency is questioned later.
- Multiple feedback strategies:
  - Implementing self-assessment, peer assessment and concept checking distributes workload and creates more independent learners.
- Receiving feedback from learners:
  - Essential for trainer improvement and creating trust in the learning environment, feedback is best collected at multiple points – near the beginning, midway and at the end of training.
  - More frequent feedback (weekly/daily) is recommended for longer courses.
- Creating a feedback-friendly environment:
  - Learners often hesitate to give feedback without being asked, and may stay silent due to fear, embarrassment or assuming they're alone in their confusion.
  - You can't assume that 'no feedback means no problems'; it's a good idea to explicitly encourage questions and feedback.
  - Learner experiences vary widely based on backgrounds, learning styles and prior knowledge.
  - Different generations may have different comfort levels with providing feedback (for example, millennials versus gen X).

Chapter 10 reflection
Check your answers to the initial pre-test (stage 4 diagnostic) – how much have you learnt? What are your biggest takeaways from this chapter? What will you do differently?

CHAPTER 11

Process feedback

The outcome

Process feedback

The why

Why is it important to process feedback?
Because if you don't, you will keep getting feedback like this:
- 'Reading out loud from textbooks is not an effective learning tool and made some people very uncomfortable.'
- 'Death by PowerPoint. We need more practical activities and videos rather than just being talked at.'
- 'I understand that training a book of rules can be challenging at times, but some variation in methods could enhance that.'
- 'The learning was very dry, not engaging.'
- 'Felt like we were studying to pass the test, not to retain the knowledge.'

These are real review comments from real learners. Yikes. Can't say I'd be thrilled to receive feedback like this – would you? These comments suggest that the trainers have not been able to learn from feedback in previous courses and have blindly just kept going doing what they've always done. The problem here?

Asking for feedback is one thing, but implementing changes based on that feedback is something else. People often receive feedback and either disregard it or never end up learning from it. The reasons for this are often that the feedback appears harsh or unrealistic, or the concerns are dismissed far too quickly as being problems that they can't, or don't have the time to, change.

A university I used to work for provides a good example here. When developing their curriculum, we discovered that the final year assessment for trainee teachers was based on the 1983 Queensland curriculum – when the soon to be teachers were studying on the opposite side of the country nearly three decades later. When questioned about the suitability of the assessment focus, the answer was, 'We simply don't have time to create a new assessment and marking criteria'.

Is that the kind of professional you would like to be known as?

Pre-test – do you really need this chapter?

The skills check and knowledge check for this chapter are in the stage 4 diagnostic on the Resources page on my website.

The 'what, when and how' (the theory)

Once you've collected your feedback, the first step is to categorise each piece as 'good', 'bad', or 'ugly'. I go into deeper explanations on what those categories mean through this chapter but, for now, it's enough to know that 'good' feedback is exactly how it sounds – things you are doing right – and the other two categories are things that learners think you can do better.

Why is it important to first categorise all your feedback as good, bad or ugly?

If you don't, you will likely:
- Read through all the feedback, and focus on the bad and ugly comments.
- Get a bit sad or peeved off, and then:
  - shove it all in a folder and conveniently forget about it

- put it in the 'too hard to deal with right now' basket
- vow never to ask for feedback again.

We've all done it. Receiving bad and ugly feedback can be a brutal exercise, but if you follow the recommendations provided in this chapter you'll soon see that all feedback can be helpful on some level, and when you 'batch' them into these categories it can be easier to learn and grow from them all.

What's the difference between good, bad and ugly feedback?

> Good question. What do you think the three categories mean? Have a quick think before reading the answers provided.

Good feedback is exactly how it sounds – things you should continue doing that your learners enjoyed and benefited from.

This is the kind of feedback that tells you how fabulous you are – it's the stuff that people comment on in the 'continue' section of the 'start, stop, continue' surveys I mention in the previous chapter. This feedback is all the things you do that work really well and are good indicators of what you should keep doing and incorporate more of. Receiving positive feedback that was a bit unexpected or surprising is also an awesome opportunity for growth. You can reflect on all the reasons that made it such a success so you can recreate that success in the future. The other awesome thing about getting positive feedback is that you can put it somewhere easy to find, so if you're ever having a bad day you can open it up and remind yourself that it's not all bad – some learners love working with you. (Don't we all need that reminder sometimes?!)

Bad feedback is the type of feedback that indicates that your learners weren't happy about something – which is often a great indicator of things you can improve on.

This is the type of feedback that really hits you in the guts when you read it – and usually because you *know* it's on point. Either you know you should have been doing it and decided it was too hard at the time, or you couldn't be bothered doing it and learners picked up on it. Ouch. But constructive feedback is a good thing. It will really help you transform your training into something better than it currently is – and it's good to get guidance on how to improve, right?

The other reason bad feedback might get you where it hurts is because you had no idea people were feeling that way and you're genuinely gobsmacked that it didn't occur to you previously. Either way, the good thing about bad or constructive feedback is that it's actually really good; it helps you transform your materials and delivery into better versions of themselves.

Ugly feedback is just that – plain ugly – and includes things that learners complain about that you really can't do anything about.

Ugly feedback includes things that are not constructive, not helpful and in no way based on things that you can, should or are able to change. This feedback might include comments about your hair colour, height, accent, age and/or nationality. (I've received ugly feedback about all these things, believe it or not!)

If you can't work out whether a piece of feedback is bad or ugly, park it for a bit. Could you look at it from a different angle? Get something constructive out of it? Maybe ask a colleague if they agree. Can they see it from a different angle? If not, ditch it – life's too short to focus on stuff you can't change!

It is, however, easy to mistake good or bad feedback for ugly feedback, which is why I often share what I think is ugly feedback with colleagues – just to 'sense check' with someone else whether I'm missing something.

I learnt this lesson in a very funny way while in Kiribati. As mentioned, I was there working on a large aid and development project setting up the vocational college to deliver accredited training from Australia. In 2010 when I was there, few exercise options for women were available, so I set up a Zumba class for anyone who wanted to join. We found a club house that had a projector screen that hadn't been used for several decades, and used that to project a DVD class. It was hilarious. So many local women turned up and were immediately such brilliant Zumba dancers. (It's a Pacific Islander thing – their collective singing and dancing skills are next level *amazing*.) Compared to the locals, we foreigners were so uncoordinated and slow to pick up the sequences that it was a bit embarrassing!

On one particular night, I was greeted by an elderly local lady who used to come to these Zumba nights regularly. I remember thinking how kind and friendly her face was, and then she motioned with her hands outstretched in front of her as if she was holding a giant ball and said something in I-Kiribati (the language of Kiribati). I gently asked the woman who was serving the drinks to translate for me. She said, 'She says you have a very big behind'.

I honestly had no idea what to say so I smiled and walked away, and, with eyebrows raised, told my friends what had just happened – unbelievable right? They agreed. The cheek! How rude! Until one of the local girls started laughing and saying, 'No, no, no. You've got it all wrong. She just paid you the best compliment ever'.

We all just looked at her incredulously. The 'best compliment'? What now? She explained that you're respected more highly if you carry weight in Kiribati because it means your village keeps you well fed – which indicates that in addition to being respected, your village is also not poor. In the *maneabas* (community meeting halls), when a large woman stands up to speak, people listen. So complimenting me on the size of my bottom was actually a way of telling me that I had her respect.

Mind. Officially. Blown.

Moral of the story? Don't disregard ugly feedback immediately – there could be an angle you're not seeing!

Demonstrate with clear examples
Shall we have a go?

> ### What would you do with feedback like this?
> These are all real examples of feedback I've received:
> - 'There are too many activities, and not enough theory.'
> - 'This is all very confusing. I don't want the theory and the examples aren't helping me. I just want you to tell me what to do to pass the assessment.'
> - 'I don't have time to watch the videos or attend the training live so this whole course is pointless. I thought there would be PDFs I could read.'
> - 'You have way too much energy – it's exhausting.'

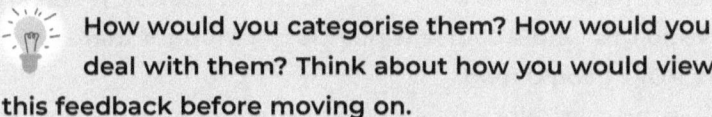 **How would you categorise them? How would you deal with them? Think about how you would view this feedback before moving on.**

You may think straight up that some of this feedback is just plain ridiculous and, therefore, 'ugly'. If you break down *why* those comments were made, though, you'll actually find that they were all examples of 'bad' feedback. They were either things I could easily change (and that could actually make the learning experience better for all of my learners), or they told me something about the learning styles of my learners.

Consider where the feedback is coming from first (this is why doing 'getting to know you' surveys at the start of a course can be so helpful!), and then decide whether the comments can be explained by the clients' backgrounds. Consider:
- previous education or qualifications
- culture, country or language
- industry, field or specialisation

- learning style and dominant 'intelligence'
- preconceived expectations regarding the learning environment.

For example, you could ask the following questions about those pieces of feedback:

- **'There are too many activities, and not enough theory.'**
  - What country or learning culture did this learner come from?
  - What was standard teaching practice in that learning culture?
- **'This is all very confusing. I don't want the theory and the examples aren't helping me. I just want you to tell me what to do to pass the assessment.'**
  - What learning styles did this learner prefer?
  - Was the class built to cater for that kind of learning style?
  - Which learning cultures was this learner accustomed to?
- **'I don't have time to watch the videos or attend the training live so this whole course is pointless. I thought there would be PDFs I could read.'**
  - Is this a learning style/time/expectations issue?
  - Apart from not being a strong audio learner, why else could watching videos or attending classes be difficult for someone?
  - Could they have a hearing impairment or auditory processing disorder? (This is me!)
  - Could they be a speed-reader who doesn't need or want to sit through hours of classes or videos if they can get the same information from a PDF? (This is also me!)
- **'You have way too much energy – it's exhausting.'**
  - Is this a learning style or learning culture issue?
  - Could it be a generational difference?
  - Could it be that they were just really tired that day?
  - Or was my energy actually over the top?

Let's have a look at how all of this feedback was actually 'bad' (things I could start or stop doing to enhance the learning experience), as opposed to 'ugly' (which they quite easily could have been classified as at first glance).

'There are too many activities, and not enough theory.'
This comment came from Japanese parents concerned that their children were having far too much fun to be learning anything. ('Fun' wasn't really the way education worked in Japan in the early 2000s.) Was this true in my culture? Nope. In theirs? Well, they'd never seen anything like it so why would they assume any differently?

When I was working in Japan, standard teaching practice was based on lecturing and rote learning, rather than critical thinking, problem-solving, group work and practical activities. Once I knew this, I could start bridging that cultural gap – could we perhaps meet in the middle? I asked the parents to join a class and explained the theory behind each 'game'. This demonstrated that it was, in fact, a learning experience – and that their children were actually enjoying it, and learning from it. Lesson learnt? Different cultures expect different things from the learning experience. Education and communication is key.

'This is all very confusing. I don't want the theory and the examples aren't helping me. I just want you to tell me what to do to pass the assessment.'
Could this comment have been from a classic kinaesthetic learner? If so, this could have been the dialogue in her head: *Stop faffing about with all this useless gaff that's just going over my head. Let me get in there and DO it, and then it will make sense. I trust you know what you're doing and the guidelines and templates will work for me. Just hand them over.*

While this could have been the case, in reality this learner came from a very different learning culture – a very academic and assessment-heavy workplace. If a learner literally just wants to do practice exams until they feel prepared, what's wrong with that? I'd prefer to have a learner doing the things they need to learn rather than the activities I had planned for the rest of the class (which I still think were great activities, just not suited to this particular learner).

Everyone is on their own learning journey. You can lead a horse to water, but it's not your job to force it to drink (certainly not if you're working with teens or adults anyway!). Adults tend to know what they need and what works for them. Listen, and embrace it – even if it doesn't make sense to you at the time.

'I don't have time to watch the videos or attend the training so this whole course is pointless. I thought there would be PDFs I could read instead.'
At first glance, I was thinking, *Well, that's the way it's delivered – so tough luck! Put some time aside and attend live or watch the video replays!*

After investigating their feedback a little more, it turned out that this learner was simply telling me that they prefer reading to watching and listening. Since it's always good to have learning materials in different formats, we ended up creating transcripts for future iterations of this course.

'You have way too much energy – it's exhausting.'
Hard to believe this could be a problem, right? This learner was indicating that my energy levels weren't matching the room. The speed at which I explain, demonstrate and present my content could, at times, get a little 'hyper' and I actually used to get this feedback a lot. #ADHDproblems.

When I first got this feedback, I was a bit gutted, then a bit annoyed, and then a bit sad. High energy is my hallmark – did feedback like this mean I couldn't be myself in the classroom?

No, that's not what the feedback was saying. After further questioning, we discovered that the learners actually *did* like the energy, and needed it in workshops that were going until 10 pm at night, but just not for two hours straight.

> So we mixed up the schedule for these workshops so that the slower, more measured co-presenter got equal air time as me, and our 45-minute sessions alternated. This way, the learners could have injections of energy followed by stretches of quiet(er) time and, over the course of a four-hour session, have enough variety to stay motivated but not get overwhelmed.

What's the moral of these feedback stories?
However ludicrous the feedback may seem at the time, there is often a good reason for it. Unless it's about the colour of your outfit, chances are it's actually feedback that can help you on some level create more options for your learners, which in turn will enhance the learning experience for a wider range of people.

Imagine a world where you ask for this feedback at the beginning of the course rather than the end (or not at all). Isn't it the perfect opportunity to get on the right page with your learners ASAP, and to make simple adjustments that provide a much better learning experience for those who learn differently?

> Don't be afraid to ask for feedback,
> and don't be afraid to act on it.

Sometimes the things that hurt the most are the things that help us the most, too!

Practical application – your turn!
Practical task 11: Process your feedback
- The next time you ask for feedback from your learners, process it into 'good', 'bad' or 'ugly' first.
- Take the bad and ugly feedback and decide whether it is, in fact, bad (indicating something you can improve), or ugly (simply unusable feedback).
- If you can't decide, or decide that you have received 'ugly' pieces of feedback, share these with a colleague for a different perspective.

- Ensure you have regular reviews built into your business or organisational model.
- Schedule how you're going to process the feedback and improve your course so that the feedback is implemented in your next review period.

Key takeaways

Here are this chapter's key points:
- Categorise feedback when you receive it. Categorising feedback into 'good', 'bad' and 'ugly' before processing it is helpful. Good feedback is positive and should be continued. Bad feedback indicates areas for improvement. Ugly feedback is unhelpful or irrelevant and can often be disregarded.
- Seek confirmation. If you're unsure whether feedback is 'ugly', seek counsel from trusted colleagues to ensure you're not missing an angle.
- Embrace all feedback. Use it to continuously strive to improve your professional practice.

> **Chapter 11 reflection**
>
> Check your answers to the initial pre-test (stage 4 diagnostic) – how much have you learnt? What are your biggest takeaways from this chapter? What will you do differently?

CHAPTER 12

Implement a reflective practice

The outcome

Implement a reflective practice

The why

What exactly is a reflective practice?

The power of reflection is enormous; it gives you the ability to work out *what* happened, *why* it happened, and *how* to prevent it or encourage it to happen again next time. It can help you make 'the positive' continue to repeat in your life, and keep the 'not so positive' firmly in the past.

Why is it important to reflect?

Once you learn to reflect and start realising how helpful it can be, it stays with you. Whether you use reflection as a way to improve your courses or delivery style, or for life in general, it's a tool that you will be able to benefit from time and time again.

Think it's a bunch of woo-woo nonsense? Okay, I hear you. Not the first time I've heard that comment. Stay with me for this next story – it's one of my most powerful teaching stories and demonstrates the power that reflection can hold.

As a teacher of reflection skills for many years, I've seen young kids turn into adults and adults uncover truths about themselves they wish they'd learnt years ago. So imagine I'm at an Australian university teaching first-year engineering and science students academic speaking and writing skills in 2007. This core unit (meaning it's compulsory for them) includes content such as giving engaging presentations, writing scientific reports and argumentative essays, and improving basic academic research skills. Reflection skills were a part of this course, with mandatory reflections as part of the assessment requirements.

Now remember, it's 2007. Engineering courses at that point were far more male dominant (this class of 30 had three females, including myself). Now imagine trying to teach reflective skills to a bunch of young Australian male 'blokey' blokes. (For the record, in 2007, Aussie men were not renowned for their ability to have deep and meaningful conversations in public about their feelings.)

Tough crowd. Not surprisingly, most of the boys were fairly reticent towards the whole process (#SoManyEyerolls) but a few did engage and start sharing their revelations in class.

The revelations were on topics far and wide, but the one that will stay with me forever was from a young male student who for the first part of the term had been quiet, introverted and unable to effectively participate in group work assignments. His reflections throughout the term had shown a deep understanding of the cycle of reflection, as he'd focused on all areas of his social and academic life, and been able to take many negative experiences and turn them into positives.

Over the term, he became a student who not only was involved in team activities but also started to voice opinions, come out of his shell and excel in group presentations. His transformation over these ten weeks was truly remarkable. At the end of the term, he handed me his final reflection, along with a handwritten letter. It read like this (shared with permission):

> Dear Maria,
> Thank you. Throughout this semester I've really developed an appreciation for reflective writing. Practising this simple technique has enabled me to look at myself and work on aspects of me that are lacking in my study and in my behaviour. What is most pleasing is that it's like going to the therapist – without the hefty price tag. I've learned so much just from this one unit of study, and the lessons gained are

going to enable me to become a better scientist and a better person too.

Last year was a weird year for me as it was the year that I told my family I was gay. This one little secret that I had kept all my life was the sole cause of so many faults and flaws I've discovered about myself. Being scared of who I am has made me really depressed and angry at times, as well as very short-tempered and sad. With this burden on me throughout my last degree, I lost focus on my study.

The reflections I've done in this unit have shed light on the fact that since I've come out I need to rid myself of these excess ill-feelings towards myself and others. I've learnt that reflective writing is a great way to express how I feel and it's a wonderful way to get rid of stress. These communications workshops are also the very first class that has enabled me to be myself and actually really enjoy learning. Even being used as a guinea pig for a classroom exercise was an experience I'll be forever grateful for as it enabled me to combat my public speaking demons. I used to hate oral presentations but now I kind of look forward to them.

At the end of it all I'm going to miss these communications workshops. I never thought I could find this unit interesting but you've made it happen for us. I made a lot of friends in this class and that's also testament to great teaching as you made us interact with each other. I've never been a people person and I've always struggled to make friends mainly due to self-esteem issues and those issues mentioned earlier, but to deal with these problems and to face them each week through doing these reflective writing exercises has been so enlightening and so helpful.

Finally after all these years of studying I can actually focus on studying and not on who I am or what I need to be; all thanks to this class – so thank you, it's been a complete life changer.

(To the learner who wrote me this reflection, I de-identified your reflection as soon as you gave me permission to use it with future groups of learners to show them the power of reflection. If you're out there and reading this, I'd love to hear from you! Reading your reflection all these years later still brings tears to my eyes!)

The power of reflection, huh? It really is one of the most powerful tools I've ever encountered in terms of being able to develop as a professional and is absolutely paramount to being able to move onwards, forwards and upwards in your own personal life journey. It's not a difficult process but once you've mastered it you can learn from any situation – positive or not so positive. Turning it into a learning experience will help you grow as a professional and as a person.

If that story didn't at least open you to the possibility that being able to reflect will literally change your life, then I get it! Reflection isn't for you! Skip ahead to the conclusion.

Pre-test – do you really need this chapter?

The skills check and knowledge check for this chapter are in the stage 4 diagnostic on the Resources page on my website.

The 'what, when and how' (the theory)

What is reflection?

It's looking at what happens in your life (be it good or not so good), and working out why those things have happened so that you can either repeat the process and keep the good things coming, or avoid the not so good things happening again.

What I've found from working in countless staff rooms and offices all over the world is that, regardless of nationality or culture, there are two types of people in the world. Developing as a professional involves being one of those two types of people – do you know which types I'm referring to?

The first type is those who know how to reflect and do it on a regular basis when problems crop up – let's refer to these people as 'reflectors'. Then there are those who simply aren't interested in going there – let's refer to these people as 'non-reflectors'.

There is no right or wrong here – it's a bit like being a *Game of Thrones* person or someone who is not interested in the slightest. (For the record, I'm not a *Game of Thrones* person.)

What do 'reflectors' do?

When you're a reflector, working with or building deep relationships professionally or personally with those who are non-reflectors can be quite difficult, and vice versa. If you do, it can often descend into chaos, misunderstandings or arguments.

Interestingly, reflectors will often unconsciously band together in workplaces, as will the non-reflectors. Not sure that's true? Fair enough! Think for a moment about the workplace you're in now or those you've worked in in the past. Think about your personal relationships as well as your professional relationships. Think about the people you've fallen out with or those who drive you 'up the wall' on a regular basis – would you say they are reflectors or non-reflectors? What would you label yourself as?

Reflectors like to go over something that happened and figure out what happened and why. They'll be curious as to what caused something to happen and whether there's a story attached that is 'behind' the obvious. If you want a funny example of this, search up the short video 'It's not about the nail'. It may seem like a funny video regarding the differences between men and women, but there's a deeper sub story there.

Now I'm not saying that women tend to be reflectors and men don't; it's more about the fact that some people want to think deeply about a situation, and others prefer to simply label it and move on.

Non-reflectors are often the type of people who have recurring patterns of behaviour – they'll do the same thing over and over, getting less than satisfactory results, and never even consider that they could be at the core of their problems.

They're also the type of professional who continually gets poor feedback, has issues with everyone else in the workplace and, more often than not, is the 'victim'. They believe they have been wronged – and definitely are not to blame for whatever negative thing is happening at the time.

If you're a reflector and something not so positive happens, you might find yourself thinking or saying (to yourself or to the non-reflectors), things like, 'Well, what are we going to do about it? What's the lesson in this? How's it going to change? What are you going to do differently next time?' From the non-reflectors, you'll be more likely to get comments like, 'I'm just unlucky', or 'I always get landed with this *[insert issue]*. It's so unfair'.

Reflectors will actively seek feedback from their learners or workplaces, they'll deal with the issues head on, and they'll become better professionals because of it. This is the core of what professional development is all about – coming to terms with the parts of your behaviour, performance or skill sets that could do with improvement and then setting about making that happen.

Is reflection for you? It simply boils down to whether you're the kind of professional who wants to keep getting better at what you do, or not. Unlike the proverbial leopard, reflectors can and often do change their spots. Non-reflectors tend not to. It's as simple as that.

What is the concept of reflection based on?

Reflection is based on this core concept: that positive thoughts create positive actions, positive actions create positive habits and positive habits create positive results. Similarly, negative thoughts lead to negative actions. Negative actions lead to negative habits and negative habits, essentially, lead to negative outcomes in general.

> **Reflection is about learning how to repeat the good things, and not repeat the not-so-good things.**

Reflection is 'deep learning', which is different from surface learning. Surface learning is like, 'Ow! I hit my toe. Ooh, that hurt … Ow! I hit my toe. Ooh, that hurt … Ow! I hit my toe. Ooh, that hurt.'

No doubt you know people like this in your life. They just continue to do the same thing again and again and again, even though they know it's not working for them. If you're a reflector, you'll more than likely be thinking, *Dude, when are you going to learn?*

Kids learn this intuitively – if they touch something hot and burn themselves, they learn not to touch hot things. Adults can somehow lose this ability as they age, as situations, relationships and consequences get more complex.

When you're a reflective or 'deep' learner, when something good happens, you can look at the process of what happened to make sure you repeat it. When something not so good happens, you can reflect on the questions, 'Why did that happen?' and 'What can I do differently next time?' This gives you the power to make different decisions the next time you are met with that situation, and turn it into a positive instead.

What is the reflective process?

If you search up 'the reflective process', you'll find lots of variations; however, they all centre on a similar theme. Let's work on the premise that reflection has six clearly defined stages. Once you get a piece of feedback or something happens to you, ask yourself:

- What happened?
- How did it make me feel?
- Was it a positive or negative experience?
- Why was it positive or negative?
- What could I have done differently at the time?
- What will I do differently next time?

Think about a recent piece of feedback that you weren't happy about. Can you run through those questions with that situation now? It can be a tricky process so let's first break down each stage in the process, before I provide a few fully worked examples.

What happened?
This is what many people (including non-reflectors) get fixated on, and never get past. The story.

If you're dealing with a less than positive piece of feedback, you can often get sucked into justifying why that feedback was given or why the learner is at fault. This is still an important part of the reflective process, and it *is* good to get 'the story' off your chest. Explain what happened. Explain the background. Explain the history. Explain the people involved. Explain everything that you can about the dynamics of the situation that happened. Be it good or bad. Then you'll be ready to move on (remembering this is just the first phase in the process).

How did it make me feel?
The second phase is where you look at how the situation made you feel – and that's not just whether it made you happy or sad, but is also deeper than that.

Does it make you proud? Positive? Negative? Ashamed? Regretful? Embarrassed? How do you feel after having been through that experience? Do you want to feel like that again, or not? Why? Is it activating something deeper in you that you need to address?

Was it a positive or negative experience?
Super simple question – isolate whether it was good or bad so that you know whether you want to repeat it or not.

Why was it positive or negative?
List out what was good or bad about it and why it was good or bad.

The point here is to really get deep down inside how that experience affected you. When you are honest about how it affected you, you can decide why you want to recreate that experience again, or why you want to avoid it next time.

How could I have made it better at the time? What could I have done differently?
You could always have made a situation better at the time in some way. And the good thing about thinking this through now is that if you ever get faced with the same situation again, you'll be prepared.

If it was a positive experience, how could you have made it even better? If it wasn't so positive, what could you have done differently?

What have I learnt from this experience that will change the way I do things in the future?

This is the most important step in the process.

It's good to recognise how you can do things differently, but it's most important to commit to *how* you're going to prevent that situation from happening again (if it wasn't positive) or ensure it *will* happen again (if it was positive).

What's the key to a positive reflection, regardless of whether the incident was negative or positive?

The key is learning from your experience – and seeing a different, even more positive future, thanks to the experiences you've been through.

When life throws you lemons? You can carry on about how bitter they are or you can make lemonade. What's your default? Carrying on or making lemonade?

Demonstrate with clear examples

Professional example – 'bad' feedback

Here's an example of going through the reflection process with some hypothetical bad feedback:

- **What happened?** My learners gave me feedback that my classes were like 'death by PowerPoint': that I was boring and they didn't really absorb any knowledge because they felt like they were just trying to pass an assessment rather than actually learn anything. The problem is my classes have so much theory to cover that I don't have time for anything other than going through all the theory, so it's kind of unfair they gave me that kind of feedback.
- **How did it make me feel?** It made me a bit angry because I try my best but the content is long, complicated and tedious – what am I supposed to do? I also felt a bit stupid because if that's what my learners are saying about me, what kind of future do I have as a trainer?

- **Was it a positive or negative experience?** It wasn't a positive review. It also made me rethink my career as a trainer.
- **Why was it positive or negative?** It wasn't good because my learners aren't engaged. They think I'm boring. The subject matter is boring. Is this really what I want to be doing for the rest of my career?
- **How could I have made it better at the time?** What could I have done differently? I actually have no idea – can I make this stuff interesting or am I doomed to get feedback like this forever? Maybe I can ask the learners for suggestions? Or other trainers who get better reviews on how they conduct their classes?
- **What have I learnt from this experience that will change the way I do things in the future?** I'm not sure yet, but I clearly need to get help in this area. I'm going to find out if a better way of delivering this content is possible by speaking to other trainers, enrolling in a teaching course or working with a teacher educator. I don't want to be known as the 'death by PowerPoint lecturer', so I will find a better way!

Professional example – 'good' feedback

And now here's an example of the reflection process with some good feedback I received:

- **What happened?** On the next page, you'll see an image of a handwritten card. I received this from a learner in an English as a Second Language class.
- **How did it make me feel?** Fabulous!
- **Was it a positive or negative experience?** Super positive!
- **Why was it positive or negative?** She felt safe and confident to make mistakes knowing she wouldn't be punished and could always improve.
- **How could I have made it better at the time? What could I have done differently?** Use her feedback to inform how I treat all students – not as a 'police woman', but as a kind and patient teacher, creating a safe space to help people build

confidence and try their hardest to improve, even when they make mistakes.

- **What have I learnt from this experience that will change the way I do things in the future?** Learners are acutely aware when they're being 'policed' by their teacher, and this creates a negative environment. Whenever I am tempted to fall into 'police woman' mode, I can remind myself it's not appreciated and instead keep providing that patient, calm learning environment where learners know they are safe to make mistakes, try their hardest and learn from the experience.

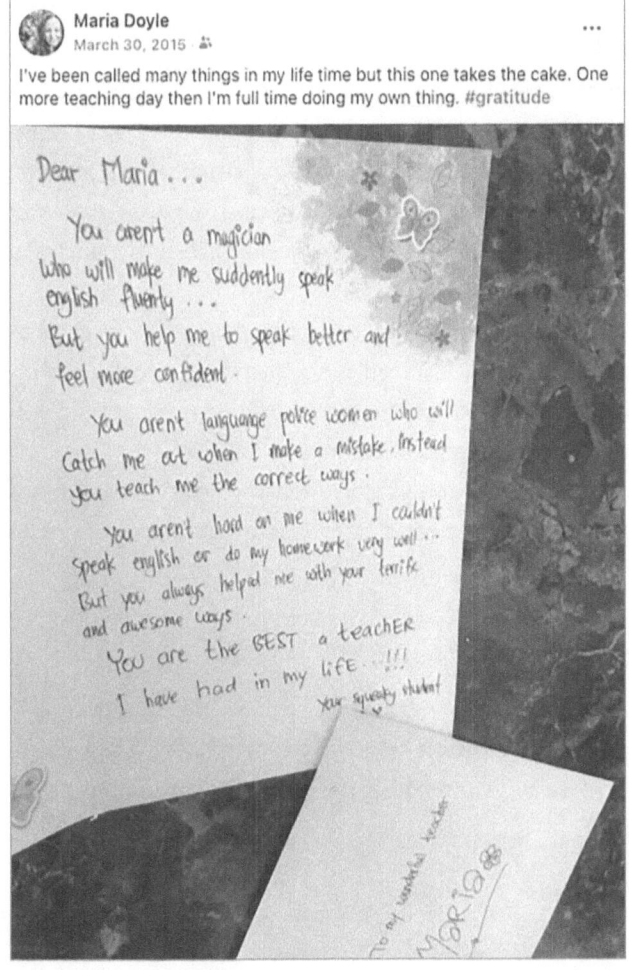

Practical application – your turn!

Practical task 12: Reflect on a piece of feedback.

Consider a piece of critical feedback you've received from a learner. Follow the prompts in the reflective process:

- What happened?
- How did it make you feel?
- Was it a positive or negative experience?
- Why was it positive or negative?
- What could you have done differently at the time?
- What will you do differently next time?

Key takeaways

This chapter discusses how to effectively handle feedback, especially in a training or educational context. Here are the key takeaways:

- Use reflective practice to process feedback. This involves analysing what happened, how it made you feel, why it was positive or negative, what could have been done differently, and what will be done differently in the future.
- Reflection is a powerful tool for personal and professional development. It helps in learning from both positive and negative experiences, and being able to make changes that help you improve as a person and as a professional.
- 'Reflectors' actively analyse and learn from experiences, and 'non-reflectors' tend to repeat patterns without learning or changing.

Chapter 12 reflection

Check your answers to the initial pre-test (stage 4 diagnostic) – how much have you learnt? What are your biggest takeaways from this chapter? What will you do differently?

Conclusion

Phew! You have a lot to think about and consider as a teacher, right? By now, I hope what you've taken from this book is that creating extraordinary learning experiences isn't just about 'fixing up' your PowerPoint slides.

In summary, you need to first CONNECT with your learners, and address what is actually needed – not what you think is needed, or what has been the status quo for years. Ask, don't assume. Flipping the narrative and making the *learner* central to the process, rather than the teacher, is the single biggest gift you can provide to any learner. Yes, you're the subject-matter expert (SME), but it's not about you – it's all about them.

Next, you need to consciously CONSTRUCT your learning experience so it motivates your learners to stay engaged in a learning journey that will see them kicking goals and changing behaviours. Having structure, and being able to provide a range of different learning products from the same IP, helps you not only tailor your learning products to the needs of the learners but also scale the number of learners you can reach. Work smarter, not harder. Systemise, optimise and digitise your expertise.

All the connection and structure in the world won't help if your slides are set up to turn you back into a lecturing machine! COMMUNICATE intentionally. Design and deliver learning materials that have a conversation with your learners, guiding them along their own discovery-based learning journey. Don't firehose your learners with information. Instead, give them what AI cannot provide – a human experience peppered with personal anecdotes and real-life scenarios that make sense in their worlds (not just a hypothetical, theoretical world). Get to know the many different 'cultures' that exist in your classroom, and co-create a safe space where learners are encouraged to 'have a go' without fear of judgement or ridicule.

All good teachers are reflective ones. We CRITIQUE ourselves, and we invite others to provide us with feedback that will help us develop as professionals. Feedback can be brutal. If confronted by feedback you've received, be open, be curious and, above all, be kind. Think outside the box. Consider the situation from all angles. Encourage different opinions, invite questions and deeply reflect on the gift of receiving feedback by committing to continuous improvement and lifelong learning.

And now, standing down from my soap box (ahem), I hope that practically this book has been useful in helping you reflect on the way you design, deliver and continuously improve your learning products.

When you next notice something isn't working the way it's meant to (indicated through low engagement, low results, or low demonstration of new skills or changed behaviour) I hope the PowerPoint presentation is no longer the scapegoat. I hope you can step back, consider the four Cs, and develop a solution that is based on the whole ecosystem, not just a single tree in the forest.

Becoming an extraordinary teacher is about relentlessly putting yourself in the learner chair and feeling the discomfort of being clueless. When you truly and regularly can relate to what your learners are feeling, you can't help but hone your own craft of being the kindest, most thoughtful, understanding, compassionate and encouraging teacher you can possibly be.

Because that's what any learner really wants and needs, isn't it?

> **They may forget what you said – but they will never forget how you made them feel.**
>
> Carl W Buehner

Carl's right.
    To learn is a birthright.
    To be human is to teach.
    You have a responsibility and a choice.

What legacy are you leaving in your family, your community and your workplace?

As you continue your journey, I'd love to hear your own teaching stories, tales of what makes the best and worst teachers all over the world – and I invite you to follow, listen in and participate on my socials.

- LinkedIn: maria-doyle
- Instagram: themariadoylestory
- Facebook: themariadoylestory

And, finally, don't forget to use all the resources I've put together for you on my Resources page, which you can access via the QR code. This page will always be freely available so share as widely as you like!

Acknowledgements

To Auntie Pam, who turned up on my doorstep with an envelope full of travel stories I'd emailed her over the years and said, 'Maria, write the book'. Thank you.

To the hundreds of international learners, friends, teachers and colleagues I've worked with over the past 30+ years, who have taught me the lessons I needed to learn, develop and grow as a teacher. Thank you.

To my original 'Giving Back Project' supporters, who backed me when I first had the idea to transform my teaching stories into something that could help create better learning experiences in far-flung places. Thank you.

To my friends, mentors, community, colleagues and coaches who have patiently stuck with me through this 12-year book writing journey – through every bright idea, challenge, edit, wobble and 'WTAF am I doing?' moment. Thank you for your patience, and deep gratitude to all of you.

To my partner Per, who stands by me unconditionally, helping me believe that I have what it takes to create a future I would never have dreamed possible. Thank you.

To Gran, who left behind a legacy of compassion, caring, curiosity and kindness. As she taught me in her own gentle ways, learners truly do blossom when learning experiences are built on her legacy. Thank you.

And, lastly, to my readers – to those who have picked up this book because you know deep down you want to be better teachers in your family, your work and/or your community. My hope is that my gran's legacy lives long in your classrooms, and that the ripple effect translates to extraordinary learning experiences becoming 'the norm'. On behalf of all your future learners, thank you for being curious and caring enough to choose this book.

About the author

Maria Doyle has collected evidence from classrooms across 30 years and from all over the world – from Europe and the Middle East, to Asia, the Pacific, North America, Scandinavia and, of course, her home country of Australia. She has worked in primary, secondary, vocational and tertiary learning environments, for small and large businesses, government and not-for-profits, and in humanitarian and aid and development contexts. She has seen education from both sides and sitting in all the different roles – not only as a teacher, teacher trainer, curriculum developer, instructional designer, examiner and education project manager, but also as a learner of languages, sewing and golf, and as a graduate of three degree programs in languages, education and international relations.

Maria's formal qualifications include a Master of International Relations (Norway), Master of Education (Australia), Cert IV TAA, Cert IV TESOL, CELTA and Bachelor of Arts (Italian and Indonesian). However, she really learnt about what makes a good learning experience through her 18 overseas postings. Maria weaves stories from these teaching and learning adventures into her speaking, writing and training, helping others create extraordinary learning experiences that engage, inspire and motivate learners to apply their new knowledge and skills in the real world. Maria believes 'death by PowerPoint', and 'tick and flick' style learning belong firmly in the past.

Maria has appeared in over 50 publications, podcasts or columns, published and presented academic papers, worked on aid and development programs run by the Australian government, been a keynote speaker at international education conferences, studied six languages, worked with over 100 different cultures and travelled through 47 countries. (Yes, she's also exhausted just reading that list and is fast coming to the realisation that her 25-year-old self should no longer be in charge of booking up her calendar with all the fun things in all the countries! Well, maybe still a few ...)

Everyone's a Teacher comes with a complimentary *Engagement Toolkit: A Facilitator's Guide to Breaking the Lecture Habit*. All profits from the book go directly to Maria's 'Paying It Forward' project, which has been running since 2011 and provides annual volunteer teacher training sessions in places that have restricted access to quality teacher education.

Endnotes

Introduction
1. Hoogerhuis, M & Nelson, B (2018), 'Why it's time to disrupt the traditional approach to L&D', Gallup Workplace.
2. Whelan, T (2018), *Deconstructing 70-20-10*, Training Industry, Inc.

Chapter 1
3. 'Meet the eight intelligences', Multiple Intelligences for Adult Literacy and Education, www.literacynet.org/mi/intro/quickreview.html.
4. 'Learning styles as a myth', Poorvu Center for Teaching and Learning, poorvucenter.yale.edu/LearningStylesMyth.
5. See, for example, 'What's your learning style?', EducationPlanner.org, www.educationplanner.org/students/self-assessments/learning-styles.shtml, and 'Assessment: Find your strengths!', Multiple Intelligences for Adult Literacy and Education, www.literacynet.org/mi/assessment/findyourstrengths.html.
6. Deshmukh, V, et al (2014), 'A learning style classification mechanism using brain dominance and VAK method in *m*-learning environment', conference paper.
7. See *The Engagement ToolKit*, available on the Resources page of my website, for a description of these activities.

WANT SOME MORE MARIA DOYLE IN YOUR LIFE?

If you got great value out of Maria's latest book, you can work further with her in a number of ways. Check out the information on the following pages or visit her website at www.mariadoyle.com. And, of course, you can follow her on Facebook, LinkedIn and Instagram.

www.mariadoyle.com

NEED A FRESH SET OF EYES ON YOUR NEXT LEARNING/L&D/TEACHING PROJECT? HOW ABOUT A SPECIALIST IN EDUCATION AND TRAINING WITH OVER 30 YEARS OF INTERNATIONAL EXPERIENCE?

Maria's ability to 'see' your project with a fresh lens is extraordinary.

She has collected evidence from classrooms across the world – from Europe and the Middle East, to Asia, the Pacific, North America, Scandinavia and, of course, her home country, Australia. Maria has also seen education from many different perspectives – not only as a teacher, teacher trainer, curriculum developer, instructional designer, examiner and education project manager, but also as a learner of six languages, cooking and golf skills, and three degree programs in languages, education and international relations.

Her experience also comes from working in international primary, secondary, vocational and tertiary learning environments, for small and large businesses, government and not for profits, and in humanitarian, and aid and development contexts. Her perspective is simply incomparable to other consultants in this space.

Maria has a unique way of working with diverse teams, and is renowned for her energy, enthusiasm and passion for turning lacklustre learning experiences into extraordinary opportunities for growth. Whatever your teaching and learning project, you can be guaranteed that working with Maria will give you incredible insights and extraordinary end products.

If you'd like to find out more about working with Maria please email
maria@mariadoyle.com

www.mariadoyle.com

NEED AN ENERGETIC STORYTELLER TO SPEAK AT YOUR NEXT EVENT?

Maria Doyle has a unique ability to read the room, weaving stories from her travels into the narrative while educating, inspiring and entertaining.

During the 30 years she's been working internationally, she's visited 47 countries, learnt six languages – and survived multiple organ failure, evacuation due to civil unrest, being detained as an illegal alien, blackmail and deportation on arrival (without any illegal or irresponsible behaviour to blame!). She's been fired for not being 'attractive enough to lure male customers' into a shop, lived in Asia for substantial periods being a large, white, single female, slept rough, eaten with presidents and built houses with villagers who had lost everything to fire. Her stories really are next level.

Maria has been told that you could hear a pin drop when she's delivering to a crowd, and routinely gets five-star reviews from her audiences. She embodies the ultimate speaker's trifecta of inviting her audience to 'laugh, cry and think', while also guaranteeing a down-to-earth approach that tailors the experience to whatever will serve your audience the best.

The topics Maria can talk about include the following:

Education and training:
- Everyone's a teacher – how to transfer knowledge with extraordinary outcomes in any learning environment
- Reinventing training in the corporate world
- Building an effective and engaged cross-cultural team
- Creating an effective intergenerational workplace
- Turning subject matter experts into extraordinary trainers
- Retaining IP before your subject matter experts leave with it.

Lifestyle:
- Lessons learnt from living, working and studying internationally
- Cross-cultural communication
- Lessons learnt from two medical evacuations and near death experiences.

To find out more about getting Maria to speak at your next event, either face to face or virtually, email maria@mariadoyle.com

www.mariadoyle.com

'Everyone's a Teacher'

WANT TO MAKE LEARNING FUN AND MEMORABLE?

If your presentations or training courses are lacking lustre, you'll likely resonate with these common struggles:

- You get a lot of blank stares, high drop-out rates or underwhelming reviews.
- Your learners aren't actually doing anything with the information you teach them – the information is 'in one ear, out the other'.
- Your learners are distracted, not paying attention, multitasking or completely uninterested.
- Your learning content is tired and showing its age, and you're not sure how to improve it.

A way forward is possible – and the solutions aren't as complicated as you might think.

If you loved the book, you'll love the workshop – which is the practical, hands-on version. The beauty of this workshop is its adaptability. We have adapted this workshop for lecturers struggling in a multicultural vocational learning environment, corporates updating a presentation on insider trading, and government departments looking to improve train driver education and community engagement strategies. We can tailor the workshop content to fit the specific context and challenges your organisation is facing. In fact, this is why this workshop packs the punch it does – because it's never the same workshop twice.

Other workshops available include:
- Making the most of an intercultural and intergenerational learning environment (for organisations with a diverse workforce)
- Making the most of your existing learning resources (for organisations seeking to upgrade a specific presentation or online course)
- Transforming Face-to-Face Training into Online Courses
- Breaking the Lecture Habit (communicative activities to get learners out of their chairs, working collaboratively, engaged and energised.)
- Tailored workshops for specific organisations and needs.

Reach out to Maria directly at maria@mariadoyle.com to discuss how we can tailor a workshop to the specific needs of your organisation.

www.mariadoyle.com

WOULD YOU LIKE TO INTERVIEW MARIA?

As well as helping people to create extraordinary learning experiences, Maria has lived, worked and studied abroad for most of her 30+ year career, and even now spends her time between Perth, Australia, and Oslo, Norway. She has a wealth of experience and engaging stories to share from her 18 overseas postings, where she's worked with hundreds of different cultures.

If you'd like to interview Maria for your media platform, the range of topics she can speak with authority about include the following.

Education and training:
- Everyone's a teacher – how to transfer knowledge with extraordinary outcomes in any learning environment
- Reinventing training in the corporate world
- Building an effective and engaged cross-cultural team
- Creating an effective intergenerational workplace
- Turning subject matter experts into extraordinary trainers
- Retaining IP before your subject matter experts leave with it.

Lifestyle:
- Lessons learnt from living, working and studying internationally
- Cross-cultural communication
- Lessons learnt from two medical evacuations and near death experiences.

Reach out to Maria directly at maria@mariadoyle.com

www.mariadoyle.com

www.ingramcontent.com/pod-product-compliance
Lightning Source LLC
Chambersburg PA
CBHW030315080526
44584CB00012B/575